Praise for Awakening from Anxiety

"No one likes to feel anxious. But what if anxiety were a path to personal empowerment instead of a cul-de-sac of despair? What if our struggles with anxiety were invitations to step into a new level of openheartedness?

"The epidemic level of anxiety we are seeing today the world over is inviting us to step into a new level of presence, according to author Rev. Connie L. Habash, LMFT, who offers her readers a new possibility: that the way forward—the way to peace and wholeness—is found in meeting the anxiety, not pushing it away. I couldn't agree more.

"With many experiential practices and tools, *Awakening from Anxiety* is that rare combination of spiritual understanding and practical, down-to-earth guidance. It is a useful manual both for beginners and those already committed to a path of awakening. The book is both comforting and encouraging."

—Jett Psaris, author of *Undefended Love* and *Hidden Blessings: Midlife Crisis as a Spiritual Awakening*

"*Awakening from Anxiety* is a profound and comprehensive guide for anyone suffering from anxiety. It is also a wonderful guide for anyone interested in awakening to a level of consciousness where anxiety simply does not exist. Simple and direct in its style, this book will be extremely helpful to a large number of people dealing with emotional issues, including anxiety."

—Leonard Jacobson, author of *Journey Into Now* and founder of the Conscious Livin~ ~~~~~~~~~

"*Awakening from Anxiety* is a thorough guide to releasing and moving beyond anxiety in its many forms, including worry, stress, fear, unease, and uncertainty. It includes very practical, helpful exercises, based on case studies and on Rev. Rev. Connie L. Habash, LMFT's lifelong personal experience—tried and true methods that work. Her conversational, down-to-earth and humorous style makes the book's deep psychospiritual truths easy to understand and apply in one's daily life. Thank you, Rev. Habash, for a book that is much needed in our increasingly stressful, anxiety-ridden, modern world. May it reach many!"

—Brad Laughlin and Leslie Temple-Thurston, authors of *The Marriage of Spirit*, *Returning to Oneness*, and *Living with Enlightenment*

Awakening

from

Anxiety

Awakening

from

Anxiety

A Spiritual Guide to Living a More Calm, Confident, and Courageous Life

Rev. Connie L. Habash, LMFT

Mango Publishing
CORAL GABLES

Cover Design: Roberto Núñez
Cover Photo/illustration: hanibacom / Shutterstock
Layout & Design: Jayoung Hong

For permission requests, please contact the publisher at:
Mango Publishing Group
2850 S Douglas Road, 2nd Floor
Coral Gables, FL 33134 USA
info@mango.bz

For special orders, quantity sales, course adoptions and corporate sales, please email the publisher at sales@mango.bz. For trade and wholesale sales, please contact Ingram Publisher Services at customer.service@ingramcontent.com or at +1.800.509.4887.

Awakening from Anxiety: A Spiritual Guide to Living a More Calm, Confident, and Courageous Life

Library of Congress Cataloging-in-Publication number: 2019905278
ISBN: (print) 978-1-64250-080-6, (ebook) 978-1-64250-081-3
BISAC category code SELF-HELP / Anxieties & Phobias
Printed in the United States of America

Throughout this book, I have used examples from many of my students' and clients' personal lives. However, to ensure privacy and confidentiality, I have changed their names and identifying information. All of the personal examples of my own life, however, have not been altered.

To all the seekers; those who seek to heal,
those who seek to know,
and those who seek to become their true Self.
You're not alone.

To my students and clients over the years—you have inspired me
to write this, and I am ever honored
and grateful to know you and to witness your awakening.

And to my daughter—may you always know
that everything you need is already within you.
Seek and you will find.

Table of Contents

Foreword

Awakening from Anxiety is an amazing book that directly addresses a growing contagion of stress, anxiety, and panic attacks. Connie is heroic in her unique approach, which can benefit people of all ages and walks of life. It is a timely work that gives the reader a way to traverse physical, emotional, and spiritual obstacles to experience a more calm and balanced state of "being."

The author gives personal examples as well as case studies of clients who have been able to overcome fear and anxiety to make changes in their lives. Connie has taken a complex subject and made it come alive to those who are new to, and those who are already steeped in, a "spiritual tradition."

Connie's unique approach to this subject is found in her insightful chapters on spiritual mistakes that can lead to more anxiety rather than that highly coveted state of "serenity." While so many are hurling themselves into practices that awaken their heart to feel the suffering of humanity, Connie warns of "compassion fatigue, which can cause physical, mental, and emotional injury."

Connie's important work is so needed in our world today where new thought and ancient spiritual principles coexist side by side, creating either expansion of consciousness or confusion. She sorts this out in a very real and practical way. What a wonderful relief to know that we don't have to achieve an image of perfection or grasp for an ideal of being a "spiritual person." According to Connie, this can only create more stress, anxiety, and even panic attacks when we don't think we are "doing it right" or aren't "good enough."

I thought this phrase from the author was brilliant: "My understanding of Spirit is that it is Infinite, Unlimited, everywhere Present, and all that Is. How can anything that has no limits or bounds be limited by our idea of a word called perfection?" The gift of this book helps me to realize that we are still okay even if we don't meet the standards of others or the goals we may have knowingly or unknowingly set for ourselves.

Thank you, dear author, for sharing the deep insights you have acquired throughout your many years of teaching, counseling, and journeying your own life's experiences. They are invaluable!

—Rama Jyoti Vernon, founder of California Yoga Teachers' Association, co-founder of Yoga Journal, and author, *Yoga: The Practice of Myth and Sacred Geometry* and *Patanjali's Yoga Sutras*, Books I and II translation.

Part I

From Anxiety to Awakening

As spiritual folks, we aren't exempt from the experience of anxiety. In fact, because we're often more sensitive, earnest beings in our endeavor to grow and awaken, we may be more prone to it.

I know—I've experienced anxiety in a variety of forms, and I've worked with many people similar to me who long to feel calm and a sense of inner peace. Who have struggled with self-doubt, lack of confidence, stress, and fear. And I have shown them a way through the anxiety to live with more ease and courage, even in the face of the fear.

This first section is an introduction to anxiety and some particulars about how it may be different for the spiritual person. I'll share with you my own journey from fear to serenity through stages in my life. Finally, you'll read several examples from my clients over the years of how they've worked through their anxiety. I think you'll find some common ground to reassure you that, indeed, you're stepping onto a path to transform that anxiety—and your life—into a more calm, confident place within you.

Introduction

The Problem of Anxiety, Especially for Spiritual People

"You gain strength, courage, and confidence by every experience in which you really stop to look fear in the face. You must do the thing which you think you cannot do."

—Eleanor Roosevelt

I Thought It Would Go Away

Anxiety is supposed to disappear when you become more spiritual. That's probably what you hoped for when you embarked on the path of awakening. You saw the Dalai Lama, advanced yogis in lotus pose, and teachers of spiritual awakening looking completely at ease and radiant and thought, "That's for me." You didn't bargain on actually feeling *more* anxiety!

Of course, you were called to explore a deeper connection to something beyond you—the Divine, as I like to call it. But perhaps you secretly hoped that by doing meditation, prayer, yoga, chanting, ceremony—whatever—you'd not only become somewhat enlightened, but that the anxiety would dissolve. You'd be overcome with inner peace, and you'd float by with that serene, "spiritual" look on your face that shows you have it all together and nothing bothers you.

Then, reality hit.

I've been there. I've put that pressure on myself to be oh-so-spiritual in order to get away from my stress, worry, and fears. And it didn't work. You're in good company if you feel the same.

But I have found something—a number of things, actually—that did make a difference with my anxiety. They can for you, too.

Before we step into this new journey together, let's take a look back, a look at anxiety: in particular, your experience of anxiety.

What Is Anxiety?

Anxiety is actually a normal human response to difficult times in life. We all experience anxiety sometimes. The Oxford dictionary defines anxiety as "a feeling of worry, nervousness, or unease about something with an uncertain outcome." The American Psychological Association adds that "**Anxiety** is an emotion characterized by feelings of tension, worried thoughts, and physical changes like increased blood pressure."

So anxiety is an emotion, everyone has experienced it, and it is also accompanied by physical sensations. Who hasn't felt some anxiety before a test, a move, a wedding day, or a speech? Sweaty palms, furrowed forehead, tense shoulders and jaw, and the desire to curl up in a ball might all be physical manifestations of the feeling of anxiety. Which ones have you had? How would you describe your experience of anxiety?

Under what circumstances do you typically experience anxiety? Uncertainty is a key element here. It is said that fear is about a present event (something happening *right now*), but *anxiety is about the uncertainty of things to come.* However, as you'll discover in this book, even in the present moment with something happening right now, fear—which creates anxiety—may not be based on actual real-time events. It's very rare that we experience true fear. Most of what we're experiencing when we say we're afraid is a flavor of anxiety.

When Anxiety Gets Bad

What prompted you to pick up this book? It may have been that anxiety is starting to get the best of you. This is when our anxiety becomes more than just occasional worry or nervousness.

Modern-day society, at least here in the United States, seems to be a pressure cooker just made for creating more anxiety and stress. What if I don't have the money to pay the bills this month? Got to look good for that presentation to the investors on Friday. I need to make a decision about selling the house this week! How will I get everything cleaned out in time for the move? My son is struggling in school—how do I help him? I've got to talk to my boyfriend about the blowup the other day, but how do I avoid setting him off? Many life stressors can contribute to our anxiety.

The real challenge is when you find anxiety accompanying you in your day-to-day life, even with little things. What to get at the grocery store can cause someone to feel overwhelmed. How will I ever get everything done tomorrow? What do I have to do to meet all our expenses? Heavy traffic and long commutes to and from work can compound our stress load. When anxiety starts to permeate our lives and we realize we're living with a low level of fear (or a not-so-low level!) most of the time, then we know it's time to do something about it.

The Psychological View of Anxiety

When anxiety becomes a disorder, it's reached the stage where it is not only permeating our lives but causing other unpleasant side effects. There may be intrusive thoughts that recur over and over—negative habits of mind. You might start avoiding situations just to avoid feeling anxiety, like turning down a date or an opportunity to give a talk at a local meet-up group. And it can cause physical symptoms such as shaking, sweating, dizziness, or a rapid heartbeat, and even manifest in a number of diseases and illnesses.

The most challenging aspect of anxiety is if it turns into a panic attack. This is the extreme form of anxiety and can result in shortness of breath and a feeling like you're having a heart attack. If you have panic disorder, it's essential that you seek a professional to assist you one-on-one and provide regular support to help you shift out of the negative trains of thought and behaviors (and the biochemical aspects) that lead up to panic attacks. This book can be a helpful adjunct to that work, but it's not going to be sufficient for that high-level kind of anxiety.

Most of you who are reading this book aren't having panic attacks, though. Your stress may feel like it's through the roof, and you're dealing with worry all the time, but it hasn't impacted you physically to that extreme.

That's where this book can truly help. And the fact that you are on a spiritual path is a huge benefit. Your faith and trust in something greater than you will help you through the anxiety to find some serenity on the other side.

The Spiritual Person's Dilemma—Spiritual Anxiety

Now, we add in our spiritual lives to the anxiety-producing mix, and things can get complicated. Because as we journey on our spiritual paths, we can find ourselves getting anxious about the process. We can find ourselves thinking, "Why aren't my thoughts calming down when I meditate?" "Am I doing it right?" "I feel like a sham for skipping two days," "I've got to keep up with everyone else in yoga class," and "I've avoided prayer for days, and now I feel bad."

You see, we tend to put the same pressure on ourselves in our spiritual endeavors as we do everything else—which doesn't help with calming that anxiety down.

On top of that, we may believe—consciously or unconsciously—that since we're spiritual, we should be beyond all that. We think we should already be more calm and confident because we're doing all the right things, or at least trying to. We create *spiritual anxiety* on top of our day-to-day worries. We're supposed to be transcending those base human emotions and simply be filled with love and light. Right?

Not exactly.

Yes, with the help of this book, your spiritual path will help you to find the way out of anxiety and the way into inner peace. But it's through a different door, and it requires a new kind of journey.

A New Journey, a New Habit

A lot of what perpetuates anxiety is habit. It's a habitual way of
thinking and reacting to life. Fortunately, habits can change:
you can create new habits that will transform the overwhelm
and stress into positive responses to your life, whatever your
life is like.

That's a spiritual journey. In this book, we will take a look at
what your habits of attention have been in your life, especially
on your spiritual path. One will reflect the other, for you know
that "As above, so below." What we experience and create
on a spiritual level affects our everyday lives, and the way we
approach our ordinary lives also impacts the spiritual.

So we're going to take a good look at your spiritual approach and
then take it deeper, because you may be a bit stuck on a level of
spiritual understanding and a way of going about your spiritual
practices that is perpetuating your anxiety. These are what I call
the mis-takes that spiritual people tend to make. They're simply
mis-takes : a misunderstanding of certain spiritual ideas that,
once adjusted, can make a world of difference not only in your
awakening process, but in your whole life and certainly in easing
the anxiety you've been struggling with.

Then, we'll incorporate some new ways of approaching
spirituality that will inform your entire life. You'll explore and
develop new skills that give you power over anxiety—seven keys
to a more calm, confident, courageous life. These approaches
will shift you out of worry, fear, and stress and give you the
confidence that you know how to deal with anxiety when it rears
its head. You'll be able to return to your natural state of ease
within: your true essence.

Chapter 1

My Story: A Journey of Transformation

"It may be when we no longer know what to do, we have come to our real work, and that when we no longer know which way to go, we have begun our real journey."

—Wendell Berry

My anxiety started, now that I think about it, back in grade school. I was "shy," or so I thought. Sure, I had friends, but I had a hard time feeling comfortable in new situations and reaching out to people I didn't know. The thing I was most afraid of was speaking in front of the class. I was extremely nervous and dreaded the funny faces that the mean boys would make at me. My hands trembled when I spoke, and I'd be anxious for days leading up to it.

I was also a perfectionist. I knew this about myself from a young age, and frankly, I rather liked it. I had a high standard for what I did and for what others did, too. I believed that it pushed me to excel. For a while, it worked. But there was a cost. My self-critical tendencies grew out of that perfectionism and fed into my teen insecurities.

An outgrowth of this was my tendency to worry. It was easier to anticipate the bad stuff that could happen and prepare for it than to envision the good. Part of me believed, superstitiously, that I could avert the tragedy if I thought about it ahead of time and prepared (have you ever believed that, too?). As you can imagine, it may have been a self-fulfilling prophecy: the bad things that I feared never materialized, but I stressed and suffered as if they had.

I realized as I grew into my twenties that the self-critical and worrying characteristics that I had honed so well needed to be transformed. They were causing me to fear new situations and inhibited me from deeper, more meaningful intimate relationships. I wanted to be more courageous and confident. And I wanted to find inner peace.

This initiated my journey into the popular personal and spiritual growth movement of the 1980s and 1990s. I went back to graduate school to study counseling psychology and began feeling more self-assured. For the most part, however, my deeper fears and worries went underground for a while.

I managed to avoid dealing with these fears head-on until I married, and a few years later, we decided to start a family. The pregnancy itself was fine. But through the trauma of the birth process—a long, hard labor that pushed me to the limits of what I thought I could tolerate in pain—the anxiety resurfaced in new ways. It was something about the pain of labor, from which there's no way out unless you get anesthesia (I eventually did the epidural), that brought the anxiety to the surface. The baby had to be birthed, one way or another. You can't just change your mind. At one point I was so exhausted and in so much pain that I was afraid I wouldn't make it.

In the end, my daughter arrived unscathed and healthy, but I was psychologically wounded. Going through the birthing experience and becoming a mother made me feel very anxious about everything, especially when it came to the baby. The pediatrician in attendance thought that my daughter had some difficulties inhaling, known as inspiratory stridor. Although our regular pediatrician disagreed later, that diagnosis put a fear for my daughter's life in my mind. We planned to have her co-sleep right next to our bed, which was important to us, but the close proximity also had the effect that I ended up waking up often to put my ear next to her chest to make sure she was breathing.

When it came time to move her to the crib in her room down the hall, the second I'd hear her crying about anything, I would fly out of bed like a gunshot and be down the hall within seconds. I knew I was overreacting a bit, but what to do about it?

I tried not to be an overly anxious mother. But I still could feel that I was more nervous about things than a fair number of other mothers.

At a certain point, I had to look at myself and my life. I realized that my fear of the unknown was pushing me to try to control everything. Controlling my daughter's life made me feel safer, but it was an illusion. It would never stop. There could never be enough control in order for me to feel that she was safe, or that I was safe.

This translated, interestingly, to airplanes. After her birth, I had a tremendous fear of flying. I couldn't get myself onto a plane until she was a year and a half old—we took a short trip down to San Diego. Every bump and jiggle made my palms break out in a cold sweat. My heart raced, and my muscles gripped in tension. I clenched my husband's hand but tried to hide it from my daughter, as I didn't want her to inherit my anxiety. But inside, I was terrified.

It was another manifestation of control, or lack thereof. I felt that if I could be in control of the flight and make it all smooth, it would be fine. But of course that wasn't possible. So anything that was outside of what I believed was safe was cause for alarm. We took another flight to Chicago later that year, but after that I avoided flying again for a few years. I knew I had to do something about it.

It was when I took the Fear of Flying Course at San Francisco International Airport (www.fofc.com) that I understood my main problem—I had to surrender. I truly had to let go of what was not mine to control. It was time to surrender it to the Divine—to something greater than me—if I was going to release this anxiety. The anxiety was all about insisting that things had to be the way I wanted in order for me to feel OK. I couldn't continue through life that way. I knew that sometimes things were going to be quite different than what I wanted, and I needed to learn to embrace that.

So my journey has been one of acceptance, presence, and surrender. I've had to use all the tools at my disposal, from my psychotherapy training to my spiritual teachers to yoga practice and philosophy. I had to reexamine my spiritual beliefs and explore them on a whole new level—again and again and again.

I practiced these tools on airplanes and as a passenger in the car. I practiced when I was taken to the hospital for an emergency appendectomy and when my daughter took her trip to DC and New York at the end of eighth grade. Many situations in life were going to bring unpredictability, and I would have to accept them. Many things could turn out to be uncomfortable and unfamiliar, and I needed a way to accept that with some grace.

Through my own inner work, I found it; not a magic pill or formula, but a continual practice that brings me back from the painful edges of anxiety to recovering my inner essence in the present moment. It is a whole practice, one that brings together every aspect of myself and my life into this simple, precious moment—with gentleness and great trust in the process.

Not surprisingly, more and more clients showed up with anxiety issues. I found that the very things that worked well for me also worked for them. Women and men who came to me with the worry, fear, and stress that was ruling their lives were finding freedom again—not from avoiding the feelings or the issues that triggered them, but from a whole-hearted, embodied embracing of themselves: a way of approaching anxiety that's sustainable, one that not only shifts us out of the debilitating suffering but opens up an entire new way of approaching life.

For years, I suffered like you. And to be truthful, I still deal with anxiety from time to time. But it no longer takes me over and rules my life. I wanted to write this book for you and the many others who, like myself, have struggled with fear, worry, stress, and overwhelm—and who long to be free of their anxiety.

Now, listen to the stories of clients, students, and friends who have found this path to releasing and transforming anxiety helpful. Picture yourself in their shoes, and envision what can be possible for you—a life of greater ease, serenity, and confidence.

Chapter 2

You Can Feel Calm, Confident, and Courageous!

"We have come into this exquisite world to experience ever and ever more deeply our divine courage, freedom, and light!"

—Hafiz

There's no question that anxiety is challenging to deal with. Fear is the biggest obstacle to living a divinely inspired life. We're all familiar with fear and how it can stop us in our tracks.

But there's hope. You picked up this book because you wanted to make a change in your life, and some part of you *knew* you could.

I want to share with you not just my story, but the stories of many others who have worked with various principles from this book over more than twenty-five years as a counselor and yoga teacher. I've also interviewed a number of spiritual people about their anxiety, what makes it worse, and what calms them.

They've struggled with many of the same things you probably do: stressed-out minds, agitated thoughts, worries about things like money, difficulties in their job, relationship challenges, social anxiety, worries about the state of the world, fear of change, self-doubt...you name it, I've probably worked with it. Read on to see that it is possible to awaken from *your* anxiety.

Anxiety from Your Past

Many of us have painful, traumatic events in our past and are still dealing with their ramifications. Anxiety often has its source in one of those past events. But it can be healed and transformed with mindful and patient application of these principles.

Lian moved to the United States from a war-torn country in Asia in her teens. As you can imagine, her childhood was difficult, and not just because of the very real danger of being killed by the fighting factions in her town. She had a mother who was an abusive alcoholic and a father who was often absent most of the year due to having to seek employment in a nearby country.

Recent triggering events in the world caused Lian's anxiety to rear its head again, and she felt like curling up into a ball on my therapist's couch. She wanted to squeeze her entire self into the core of her body and visualized covering it with a very hard, thick shell.

As we practiced the techniques in the chapters "Feeling Your Anxiety" and "Listening to Your Anxiety," she was able to dialogue with the "hard shell." She expressed appreciation for its desire to protect her, and she listened to what that part of her needed.

Breathing into this, her body softened, and she noticed that her neck and shoulders relaxed more. She felt very tired and even dozed off for a moment—the armoring let go enough for her to feel safe to fall asleep, right there on the couch! While working together over a period of time, Lian became more and more skilled at embracing her anxiety, moving through it, and transforming it.

Needing to Control

Carla—who you will read more about later in this book—was a diligent, hardworking real estate professional and had a family to care for as well. She came to my yoga classes and teacher training to expand her horizons and feed her soul. As we explored yoga philosophy more deeply, she realized she had control issues that caused anxiety and hindered her ability to feel inner peace.

Even though she didn't consider herself religious, she found that she could have a spiritual practice that surrendered everything over to the Universe. Using some of the principles in the "Surrender" chapter, when she felt overwhelmed by life's demands, she would "take all that anxious energy, visualize releasing it into the universe, and trust that everything would work out." She felt comfort in the fact that whatever was going to happen was meant to be. "I truly felt myself give up control. I have a newfound sense of peace that comes from allowing myself to give up control and completely trust that whatever happens was meant to happen. My anxiety has decreased significantly, and when I do begin to feel overwhelmed, all it takes is a quick reminder to just let it go."

Gratification, Impatience, and Trust

Impatience and difficulty delaying gratification are common triggers of anxiety. Holly could relate to that. She found that when she couldn't get something instantly, she tended to think about it a lot. This led to worry and anxiety. Holly didn't feel as "in control" of her thoughts as she would like. "If I can't see how it will be, how it can change, or what the outcome might be, it triggers anxiety."

After reflection and years of working on her inner healing process, Holly realized (much like Carla) that it's "a fallacy to believe I can control everything." She developed more trust and was able to wait more patiently for things to unfold. In another example of the power of surrender to transform anxiety, Holly learned to appreciate and accept things as they are for now, and to be more present in the moment (see the upcoming chapter "Presence"). "I think that is what is meant by Grace."

Anxiety and Highly Sensitive People

Many of us on the spiritual path are "Highly Sensitive Persons," or HSPs. According to Dr. Elaine Aron, author of the national bestseller, *The Highly Sensitive Person*, HSPs tend to be easily overstimulated (and thus anxious), have finely tuned empathy, process deeply, and are sensitive to subtleties, such as shifts in other people's mood or energy. Melissa definitely qualified, and anxiety had been a lifelong challenge for her.

Melissa tended to feel everything—her own emotions, which were deep and intense, and everyone else's, too. It was difficult to distinguish her feelings from those of others. She also had a low tolerance for incongruity: when people said one thing and did another, it troubled her. She could feel the truth of the situation, but others would deny it, even when it was apparent. Additionally, Melissa compared herself to others frequently, compounding her anxiety and undermining her confidence.

Melissa began shifting out of anxiety by being conscious of how and where she placed her attention. Working with the practices in the "Embodiment" chapter (especially Me/Not Me and maintaining healthy energetic boundaries), she was better able to navigate the world and other people's emotions without being triggered into fear and worry.

Avoiding Feelings vs. Sitting with Them

Elisa was another yoga student of mine who had a lot of stress and anxiety in her life. She found that she tended to cope with the stress, as many of us do, by overeating or having a glass of wine. But she knew this wasn't solving the problem, just avoiding it.

Elisa found a way to shift the anxiety by coming deeply into the present moment with the feelings within her (and you will, too, in the chapters on "Presence" and "Feeling Your Anxiety"). When the emotions arose, she practiced sitting with them rather than avoiding them. "When I do stop, I find that, like everything else, negative feelings pass. Both meditation and yoga are useful tools to sit with negative feelings until they leave." This not only calmed her anxiety but built her emotional resilience, leading her to insight and growth.

Sonya M. Kelly, PhD, psychologist and author of the book, *Meditative Visualization: How 2 Minutes A Day Can Change Your Life*, developed anxiety in her childhood and similarly learned to cope with food. She grew up through the stress of her parent's relationship problems, separation, financial difficulties, and sexual molestation. Food was a comforting coping mechanism.

Through her years of personal and spiritual growth, she found a way to transform her anxiety into courage and strength, rather than avoiding it through overeating. By opening to the Divine Source through meditation, she increased her emotional resilience. She allowed the emotions inside to arise in her meditations and experienced cathartic releases, which can also be achieved using the practices we will explore with *feeling* and *listening* to your anxiety. Dr. Kelly also found that empowering actions—being afraid and taking action anyway—were pivotal in overcoming the fears that beset her. You'll discover more about empowering actions later in this book, including how you can use them to shift toward courage and calm.

Divorce and Anxiety

Many of us go through relationship breakups and divorce. Even the most amicable divorces are difficult; and the contentious ones can trigger constant worry and fear.

Renee came to see me as she was going through the ups and downs of the divorce process. Although the paperwork, legal proceedings, shuffling the kids back and forth, and dealings with her ex were plenty stressful, what triggered her anxiety the most was being alone and fearing that she wouldn't meet another man to share her life with. She also was prone to criticizing and blaming herself when things went wrong, which hindered her ability to trust the process and to believe she could find the relationship partner she dreamed of.

As we worked with the fears and self-doubt that arose in the process of healing, Renee cultivated the skill needed to hold her feelings with awareness and compassion (coming up in the chapter "Self-Compassion"). She let go of the anxiety-provoking stories she habitually told herself about why people acted the way they did. Through engaging in this process, she not only was better able to move on from her ex-husband, but her self-confidence increased. Renee learned to love herself as she was and to trust in the Divine (more on that in the "Surrender" chapter); soon, she began to date again.

Fear of Rejection

A very common source of anxiety is the fear of being rejected, judged, and shamed. Perhaps we grew up with critical, shaming parents, or were mocked or ostracized at school, and that experience carried forward into our adult lives. This fear can become an unconscious motivator—or hindrance—in our daily lives, as well as a source of perpetual anxiety.

Anne was no stranger to this. She struggled with generalized anxiety most of her life, primarily related to fear of rejection. She was always "trying to do the right thing, keep the peace, and accommodate everyone around me. I even play the part of a person who is 'easygoing, relaxed, and mellow' as my friends typically describe me. But as my attuned husband tells it, I am like a duck in the water: calm, serene, and peaceful above the water, but with feet churning ferociously underneath to stay afloat."

Few others knew how much she suffered, but she was keenly aware of how the anxiety afflicted her life. Through the application of yogic principles and the ability to witness her thoughts and emotions from a more neutral place (more about that in the "How You Do Spirituality is How You Do Everything" chapter), she felt "better equipped to deal with them." "To be able to identify it, label it, observe it, and have a thoughtful reaction to it is empowering."

It's Time to Get Started!

You're in good company—many before you have embarked upon this journey of awakening from your anxiety. The clock has sounded, and now you're arising out of bed, ready to take on the new day of living with more calm, confidence, and inner peace. Turn the page, and let's get started!

Part II

The Mis-takes Spiritual People Make That Perpetuate Anxiety

We've all done it. With the best of intentions, we set out on our spiritual path, ready to have our awakening and determined to find the calm, centered, peaceful place within that is beyond our anxiety.

Often, we do find that place—for a while. It's the natural cycle of things for this state of being to come and go. When that calm, courageous place within begins to slip away, we might make some spiritual mis-takes .

They can be errors in our approach, perspective, or how we're applying our beliefs. These spiritual mis-takes —for they're just slipups, missing the target we're trying to achieve—aren't a big deal. We all get a little off track sometimes.

The problem is that we tend to *make* them a big deal. They can become deal-breakers, sending us down the spiral of not only more anxiety, but self-recrimination and anxiety *about* our anxiety.

Let's take a look at some of the most common mis-takes on the spiritual path that can get under our skin and actually perpetuate that anxiety—which is not what we want to have happen! Then we'll chart a correction on our course and dive into the keys that will release us from the anxiety cycle.

Chapter 3

Spiritual Mistake #1 Perfectionism

"Let go of who you think you are supposed to be so that you can be who you truly are."

—Brené Brown

I'll bet you weren't at all surprised to see this as my number one spiritual mistake. Chances are good that you're a perfectionist (or like me, a recovering perfectionist!).

We often embark upon practices like yoga, prayer, or meditation because we're hoping for a perfectly peaceful life. And then remember the last time you sat for meditation and it was crummy? All kinds of distracting, anxious, upsetting, annoying thoughts were going on. Did you say, "yippee"? Or did you get frustrated? Of course, like me, you were probably quite displeased.

Maybe you then tried harder to push those thoughts away, thinking, "This is not supposed to happen! I am supposed to be calm, relaxed, and serene. I'm supposed to look and feel like a Buddha in lotus pose: eyelids half-closed, body upright and aligned but oh so relaxed, and hands in a perfect mudra, completely still, looking as if I could float on a lotus leaf. Or at least I *should* feel that way."

Um, no. Well, you certainly *can* have that experience. But if you're attached to it—attached to outcome, expecting that it should, must, has to, and needs to be that way—then you're holding on to some degree of perfection.

Spirituality Is Messy

The honest-to-goodness truth is that spirituality is a messy journey. You'll have to get used to getting dirty, digging down deep, bumpy trails, picking up the trash, and sometimes even sitting in it because it just happens to be there.

The spiritual path is not about avoidance—avoidance of anything less than ideal—but about fully embracing who you are and whatever *is*. Yes, it involves taking appropriate action to continue on the path, but still, the path is what it is.

Your mind isn't always going to be still. Neither will your body. In fact, they rarely will be. That's OK. And your anxiety will arise from time to time, even after you've been practicing meditation, breathwork, or yoga for years. But as you continue on, you'll develop the skill and courage to know how to journey through it rather than trying to push it away.

The "Saint Syndrome"

One of the attractive qualities of the spiritual path is the idea of becoming perfect. Sure, almost everyone has some ideal they seek to realize, even if they aren't spiritual, like the pinnacle of their career, winning a marathon, or writing that bestselling book.

But spiritual seekers take that to the nth degree. This is what I call the *Saint Syndrome*. We have these spiritual teachers or gurus we look up to who seem to have it all together. They're completely at ease all the time, sit in meditation for hours, seem content to continually do selfless service, and appear to have all the flawless answers to every deep question. Their love and devotion to the Divine are impeccable, as is their behavior. We look at the masters, like Jesus, Buddha, or Krishna, or modern-day saints like Mother Teresa or Gandhi, and think that we're expected to become like that. We try to mold ourselves into that serene and elevated state. Those saints certainly don't have anxiety, do they? There's an expectation to become like a saint, and we think that's the intended end result of our practice.

Do you have *Saint Syndrome*? Well, let me reassure you that you aren't expected to become one. In fact, it would be completely inauthentic to force yourself to try to be some external idea of what perfection is. Forcing yourself to be anything, even if you *think* it is your Divine nature, is simply doing violence to yourself.

Expectations

We develop this *Saint Syndrome* by comparing ourselves to others and having expectations of how both we ourselves and the spiritual path should be. Whenever expectations and comparison rear their heads, you can bet that anxiety and stress will be arriving in short order.

When I was nineteen, I took my first personal growth workshop at the encouragement of my father, who was very much into the self-improvement movement. In that first course, I learned something that stuck with me the rest of my life: *expectations lead to disappointment.*

When we have an expectation that something will happen in a certain way, i.e., attachment to outcome, we're setting ourselves up for feeling let down. This is not the same as having a goal or an intent. We can have a clear idea of what we want to achieve or how we want to feel, like more relaxed and at ease. But if we're expecting that result all the time, or expecting that at some point we won't have to deal with fear or worry anymore, and then they show up, we can fall into the downward spiral of self-recrimination, shame, despair, and doubt.

We do our spiritual work (or play!) in order to increase our capacity for love, peace, trust, clarity, resilience, and many other qualities, and to improve the state of our lives. But if we have expectations about how that ought to unfold or what that looks like, and it doesn't turn out perfectly that way (hint: it probably won't), we're setting ourselves up for more anxiety.

Case Study: "Why Did I Lose My Calm?"

Marilee came to see me for difficulties with anxiety and depression. She struggled with being able to keep it all together: being a mom of three kids and a devoted wife, and at the same time, holding down a rewarding position as a social worker for a county clinic that served at-risk adolescents. She felt good about making a difference for these teens and loved her family, but often felt it was more than she could handle. She believed she was falling short of what she thought a mother, wife, and social worker should be.

I helped her return to her spiritual practices of meditation, self-compassion, and mindfulness, and, as we worked together for some time, she developed more ease and calm in dealing with her daily life. Her consistent practice was paying off.

Marilee planned to visit a spiritual center in Europe where there was a meditation teacher she admired, and that involved travel and flying. Fear of flying had been one of the issues for which she had sought help. She prepared, and she felt she was ready to travel, armed with the serene state she was developing.

But a wrench was thrown into the plan. She had to take a couple flights to get to her destination in France. The first one was the most turbulent flight she had ever experienced. She white-knuckled through it in a state of sheer terror. Then, on her connecting flight, she encountered a long delay, during which the passengers had to sit inside the airplane on the tarmac for hours—on a blazing hot day. She felt claustrophobic and panicky. This was not turning out how she had planned! And try as she might, she just couldn't implement her mindfulness practice—it was just too scary. When she finally arrived at the retreat center, she felt traumatized. Although she enjoyed being there, it didn't pan out to be the experience she had hoped it would be.

Coming home still feeling shook up from her ordeal, she despaired, thinking, "Why did I lose my calm state I had worked so hard to create?" She felt dejected and resistant to meditating again, with "Why bother? What did I do wrong?" going through her mind.

What I helped Marilee see is that no matter how much we prepare, sometimes life happens. Our spiritual path isn't about meditating for a while and becoming perfectly serene, and then everything else is cake. The practice is to let go of our expectations and perfectionism and to know we have the resilience and skills to endure the challenges and return to our center again. She didn't do anything wrong, other than the mistake of believing she wouldn't have to feel fear again. After some work with self-compassion, feeling and listening to her anxiety, and embracing the *now* by letting go of how it was before (all of which is coming in Part III), the tension and despair released. She returned not only to feeling ease within, but also to her meditation practice—with nonattachment to outcome!

The Trap of Comparison

Comparison is related to expectations. I've often told my clients, "Comparison is the root of all depression." When we compare ourselves to someone else—whether to a saint or that gorgeous woman in the sexy yoga clothes perfectly balanced in Crane pose on the mat next to us—we're bound to feel less-than, as well as more anxious.

Comparison is a trap both ways. If we think, "Hey, look at me—I can sit still longer than those two guys over there who keep fidgeting...aren't I a great meditator," then we're setting ourselves up again. Because we can be sure that comparison is a pendulum. If we're feeling up and better-than one minute, then the next minute or the next week we'll swing back into the doldrums. It's the tricky ploy of the ego to try to keep us engaged in perfectionism by comparing, so that we'll need that ego constantly telling us how great we are. If we fear not measuring up to others, we'll get attached to feeling superior in order to compensate, and then we're stuck in that comparison trap.

The last thing we want is to feel crappy about ourselves, isn't it? But that is where the pendulum eventually swings if we buy into feeling that we're better than others. The way out of the comparison trap is to let go of both ends of the spectrum: neither indulging in superiority nor allowing ourselves to believe that we're less-than. The truth is that we are worthy, good-enough people and have been since the day we were born (and even before that, if that fits your beliefs). The simple fact that you came to this planet means you're valuable and have something to offer. Let go of comparing yourself to others and trying to be perfect, focus on what you have to offer and who you truly are, and you'll find your worries and fears diminishing.

Intolerance

Perfectionism causes anxiety because we become intolerant. OK, this is not a commentary on social justice. This is a commentary on how intolerant we become of ourselves and our lives when we buy into the idea that there's some perfect way to be.

Spirituality ups the ante on our idea of perfection, because now we not only have to *do* something perfectly, we expect ourselves to be a perfect *soul*. Saint Syndrome tells us that we must not feel, think, or act in any way other than that of a blissful, transcendent yogini.

This attitude is terribly intolerant of, uh, *human beings.* All emotions are part of the experience, and worked with consciously, even the so-called "negative" emotions, like anger or fear, have gifts for us (as you'll see in the section "Empowering Action"). Human beings make mis-takes , spill the milk, fart, and leave their desks messy. We also may react at times when we wish we would have responded.

The spiritual path is intended for imperfect people, because it's those foibles and challenges that help us grow. We develop more compassion and open our hearts by our willingness to be vulnerable and embrace the pain and suffering of life. This takes us much deeper in our awakening than acting perfect all the time. So please, my friend, be more tolerant of yourself.

Perfection Is a Human Invention

The bottom line is that there's really no such thing as perfection. Perfection is a human invention. It's an idea conceived of and defined by human beings with limited human minds.

We have this idea that perfection means that everything is completely right and unmarred. Someone who is perfect has no flaws. We believe that it's possible to be that perfect person. And we project this idea on our concept of the Divine, too—that *It* is perfect...according to *our ideas* of what perfect means.

But my understanding of Spirit is that it is Infinite, Unlimited, everywhere Present, and All That Is. How can anything that has no limits or bounds be limited by *our idea of a word called perfection*? And if that is true—that perfection doesn't exist, not in the way we conceive of it, in the realm of the Infinite—then why are we as spiritual seekers holding on to the idea? Why hold onto an idea that causes us anxiety from continual self-comparison and, naturally, falling short?

Furthermore, if perfection doesn't really exist except as a ridiculous idea in our minds, then neither does imperfection. Step out of the duality of perfect/imperfect and simply allow yourself to *be*, right here as you are. Take a deep breath of appreciation for simply *being*. You might find just by doing that, your body and mind relax a bit—one step made on your journey to more ease and resilience.

Chapter 4

Spiritual Mistake #2
Flight to Light

"Avoidance is the best short-term strategy to escape conflict, and the best long-term strategy to ensure suffering."

—Brendon Burchard

Back in the 1980s, when I first embarked officially on the spiritual path, it was the "New Age." Channelers, crystals, tarot cards, and "the Harmonic Convergence," a rare astrological alignment, were all the rage. A common theme that emerged during that time was "going to the Light."

It's a projection of the perfectionistic mindset of a spiritual seeker. Don't feel anger or any of those "dark" parts of yourself (notice any judgment there?), just go to the Light. Surround yourself in Light, and push all those bad thoughts away. Live in the Light, and everything will be blissful. Everyone was running as far as they could from anything that could be seen as dark and *unspiritual*. This tendency to avoid the Shadow, the less-than-desirable parts of ourselves, and cling to our imagined ideal was known to some of us as "Flight to Light."

It works really great—until you blow up at your kid or someone cuts you off on the freeway, or a deep-seated fear arises from within us, and suddenly the Light isn't working to make it go away.

Everything Isn't "All Good"

We can't transform our fear, pain, and worry by pretending it doesn't exist or matter. The more modern version of the Flight to Light is "It's All Good." There's good intent behind this statement—we can certainly choose to see the good, the helpful, and the transformative aspects of our most unpleasant situations. But when someone else does something that triggers our anxiety, one can't make it all better by just saying "It's All Good." Running to the light side of the situation too quickly avoids the potential for some deep healing of our worst triggers.

In my experience, it's better to acknowledge that something doesn't feel so good, or that we're not happy with a behavior that's emerged in us, especially when we're reacting out of fear. We can acknowledge it without indulging in it, and we can help ourselves to heal and release the fear by moving through it rather than pasting a pleasant face on the pain.

When someone is trying to look calm and loving when you feel that there's something else brewing beneath the surface, you notice the dissonance. It's inauthentic. We have a hard time trusting someone who says and does all the right things but does them with clenched teeth in their tight smile, and who might occasionally have a sharp retort or a short fuse when the image they are trying to hold is just too much.

Avoiding the Shadow and Spiritual Bypassing

The people who indulge in Flight to Light avoid the Shadow— that unconscious part of personality known as our "dark" side.

But it's not limited to the uncomfortable, unpleasant aspects of the self. The Shadow also contains good qualities that we don't perceive we possess. Essentially, the Shadow holds all that we aren't willing to look at within ourselves—and that's often the "negative" qualities. We shove our insecurities, less-than-desirable traits, and shame and self-blame, among other disconcerting aspects of ourselves, into the closet of the Shadow, and then lean back against the door to attempt to keep it closed—tight.

A related idea that falls under the Flight to Light category is *spiritual bypassing*. According to Robert Masters, author of *Bringing Your Shadow Out of the Dark*, spiritual bypassing "is the use of spiritual practices and beliefs to avoid dealing with our painful feelings, unresolved wounds, and developmental needs." Anything that we're afraid of looking at and owning is passed by—shoved back into the Shadow indefinitely.

We think that we have just gotten rid of the anxiety that we judge as pathetic, or our anger that is so "unspiritual," by sweeping it under the rug. But we know deep down inside that it ain't goin' away. It's just piling up inside until the time when it can't stay hidden anymore.

What You Resist, Persists

You know the old adage—what you resist persists. Or, whatever you push away is going to stay. This is why Flight to Light is problematic. By resisting an issue, a feeling, a thought, or a behavior, we actually give it power. It's like an old, festering wound. When it's raw and small, you can deal with it pretty well. You grit your teeth, pour the burning alcohol over it, and cleanse it. But if you avoid the sting of having to clean the infection, it starts to grow and can develop into a serious condition.

When we try to push away our anxiety and the sources of it, we shove it into the unconscious. There it can grow into quite an unmanageable beast, which makes us avoid things in life that could be satisfying. We begin to feel nervous or uncomfortable. If we do that for a long time, the fear starts to have control over our lives.

Pushing a Wall

Using a metaphor of a wall is another way to understand why resisting is problematic. Imagine that the wall has something on it you don't like—maybe a mark from a piece of furniture that banged into it. That mark represents a character trait you don't like about yourself, or an emotion you don't want to deal with or confront; say, anger. Go ahead and push that anger away. Push on the wall where that mark is, as hard as you can. Go on, keep doing it. Going anywhere? Is the anger disappearing? How do you feel? Probably tired at some point, yes? Frustrated? It's silly (and needlessly exhausting!) to try to make a mark on the wall disappear by pushing it away, isn't it?

When you repress things like anxiety or anger into the Shadow, it's like that. You can't pretend you're not angry when you are. It will take a lot of energy to try to repress something like that. It won't make it go away, and you'll just deplete your energy. Walls are walls, and we can't make a spot on them disappear by trying to shove it away.

Now, instead, just look at the mark on the wall. Get to know it. How long is it? What is its shape? How do you think it got there? Can you wash some of it off? Step back. Look at the spot again, and the whole wall. Step back even farther. What do you notice? Do you see that it's just a small part of the wall, probably? If you stood all the way on the other side of the room, can you even see it? Maybe, maybe not. Now, what if you walk away? Once you have consciously acknowledged the spot, you can do that, and now your attention isn't on it. It's still there, but you haven't denied the fact, and you're not fighting against it. You could even decide to paint over it at some point, but that comes from acknowledging that it is there, recognizing that something needs to be done about it, and taking appropriate action—not trying to push it away.

Resistance Creates Anxiety

If you're resisting your own fear, worry, and stress, you're not alone. Many of us would simply like for it to go away. But resisting it not only stockpiles it inside of you. It creates tension and depletes your energy in order to keep those feelings underground—which also creates *more anxiety*.

If we believe the ideas that 1) this feeling is too much, too uncomfortable, and/or too scary to feel and that 2) getting rid of it makes us feel safer, then we'll become obsessed with trying to get rid of it, won't we? When our anxiety arises and we're buying into these two beliefs, we'll do everything we can to avoid it and feel more secure when we successfully do so.

But when we aren't successful at pushing it away and sweeping it under the rug, we'll become more anxious than before: "Oh no, I just can't get rid of this, and it's too awful for me to tolerate, and I'm not in control of it, so this is really, really, really awful!!!" Attachment to avoiding anxiety increases the very thing we're trying to rid ourselves of. Flight to Light perpetuates fear of anything labeled "not-Light"—including our fears themselves.

So the practice of truly transforming our anxiety—turning the unwanted food scraps and garbage (i.e., your worries and stress) into desirable compost and soil (spiritual awakening)—can only happen when we consider that feeling the anxiety (or any other "negative" emotion) might be OK. We increase our tolerance and resilience in the face of it, and we let go of trying to hide or control it. Don't worry, I have a plan in Part III that will help you be able to do that successfully. You can return yourself to the inner peace that was yours from before you were born.

The Transformational Power of Those "Negative" Emotions

So-called negative emotions, like anger, hate, fear, jealousy, etc., have power in them. If you just gloss over them and run to the positive—the "Light"—you'll miss a big opportunity, because they are essential for spiritual and personal growth.

Fear brings to our awareness what lies outside of our comfort zone and what we have allowed to have power over us in some way. Anger clarifies what truly matters to us, calls us to set boundaries, and gives us the vital energy to speak up to take necessary action. Any emotion that we might label as "negative" can be understood in this new perspective. Worked with on a conscious level, you can walk through the dark or "Shadow" side, claim the treasures of healing and empowerment, and come out on the other side no longer at the mercy of those feared emotions. That will definitely reduce anxiety and build your courage muscles. I'll detail how to use anxiety to empower you in Chapter 15, "Empowering Action."

Rather Than Splitting Off the Dark—Wholeness

Wholeness is essential to the spiritual path and to overcoming our fears, for at the roots of anxiety is trying to split off what we're frightened of or uncomfortable with inside ourselves. The path of healing and awakening is welcoming it all back in while knowing we are capable of being with it. This takes time and practice with the techniques I share in this book, but it is definitely possible. Rather than chopping ourselves and our experiences of life into acceptable and unacceptable pieces, we learn to love the whole of ourselves unconditionally and to embrace life with whatever appreciation and acceptance we can muster.

In yogic philosophy, two of the five causes of suffering are *raga* (pronounced RAH-guh), or "attachment," and *dvesha* (pronounced DVAY-shuh, with "dvay" rhyming with "bay"), or "aversion." This is the dance of the Flight to Light and avoiding our Shadows, and it is a source of our afflictions.

Yoga philosophy also gives us a wonderful practice to help us out of these problems with avoiding the dark material. It is known as *upeksha* (pronounced like oo-PAKE-shuh, rhyming with "take"). This roughly translates as "even-mindedness." When life is good, we can be happy and appreciate it, but stay even-minded and not become overly attached to it. When life is difficult, or when we encounter situations, people, and aspects of ourselves that we judge as "bad," negative, or even wicked, we need even-mindedness all the more. It is the ability to step back and see what *is* without reaction, assumptions, jumping to conclusions, or blaming ourselves or anyone else.

Even-mindedness helps us to accept the unacceptable without condoning it. We can still take action to work with our less-than-desirable selves and help those aspects heal and transform. We may still feel called to help right the wrongs we see done in the world. During our current times, the Shadow may seem to be looming larger than ever. But it's important not to give in to the fear and run away. *Upeksha* helps us stay steady and aware without reacting so that we can respond effectively to whatever provokes our worries. We can remain rooted in our inner calm, even in the moments when the dark seems to overtake the light and our anxiety rears its head.

Chapter 5

Spiritual Mistake #3
Leaving Your Body

"It is only by grounding our awareness in the living sensation of our bodies that the 'I am,' our real presence, can awaken."

—G.I. Gurdjieff

Often, a spiritual person may find comfort in out-of-body experiences, spending time up in the head (in thinking, imagining, and visioning), and going to other dimensions or divine realms. I consider all of these some form of leaving your body.

There certainly are benefits, both spiritual and psychological, to leaving the body. It can temporarily relieve some of the anxiety that troubles us, and these experiences can be inspiring and awaken us to transcendent realities. When we're being creative, whether dancing, painting, singing, or writing, we often tap into other realms and allow them to be expressed through us. Experiencing an altered state of consciousness can be a positive and life-changing experience. Leaving your body, whether literally or in the imagination, can help us to gain perspective to be able to step back from ourselves and see our situation differently.

Dissociation

From the psychological perspective, leaving the body is referred to as dissociation. Much of what I'm talking about isn't clinical dissociation, though. Many of us experience a bit of dissociation. The Sidran Institute, an organization dedicated to helping people understand, manage, and treat trauma and dissociation, defines dissociation as "a mental process that creates a disconnection between a person's thoughts, memories, feelings, actions, or sense of who he or she is." Daydreaming, becoming lost in a book or a movie, or driving down the highway and realizing we have lost awareness of what we passed are all examples of mild, common dissociation.

Dissociation often kicks in when we're faced with trauma or situations that cause us great anxiety. In the moment, just as in a car accident, it can assist us in dealing with a frightening, painful, shocking event so that we can get to safety or get medical care for our injuries. It's a defense mechanism to help us get through situations in which panic would likely reduce our chances for survival.

If we were abused as children, or even at other times in our adulthood, we may have employed dissociation in order to survive through those traumatizing times. It may have felt unsafe to be in the body, and dissociation, to some degree, may have become our go-to defense mechanism. Then as we grow up, we might begin to employ dissociation any time we're faced with something uncomfortable. This can become an unhealthy pattern.

Enter Out-of-Body Experiences

If we have found dissociation to ease our fears and distance ourselves from them (another subtle method of Flight to Light), discovering that many spiritual practices encourage some form of leaving the body or spending time in visualization can seem like a boon. Hooray, I can spend more time in some beautiful, transcendent experience and out of this painful, frightening world and body! We may feel we've found paradise in the spiritual realm.

However, if we are habitually depending on leaving our body in order to deal with stress, anxiety, and upset, we move into the realm of unhealthy dissociation. In the long term, this is likely to increase anxiety.

Nobody Home!

Here's why leaving your body backfires as a way of deflecting anxiety. Think about a young child, maybe a toddler. Toddlers need to stay very close to their primary caretakers (usually, but not always, their mothers) in order to feel safe. They may test the waters and walk away a bit, but they always want to be nearby so they can come back to their mothers and receive physical contact and the reassurance that they are safe.

Imagine what would happen if you left a toddler alone in the house for fifteen minutes or an hour. How would they respond? They'd likely panic: "Nobody's home! Where is mommy? What is this world where I'm all alone? Am I safe?" Of course, we wouldn't do that, would we? It would be child abandonment. The toddler could encounter all kinds of dangers and hurt herself, or even die. Somebody needs to be home and nearby to protect, soothe, and calm her.

When you leave your body to escape what you're feeling, especially habitually or for extended periods of time, your body feels like that toddler: "There's nobody home here! No one is here to make sure I'm safe, to take care of any threats that could show up, to deal with this project sitting on my desk, to make sure the doors are locked before bed, or to look after the kids, etc." Your body quite simply freaks out.

And what happens when the body is freaked out? The nervous system—specifically, the sympathetic nervous system, which is responsible for the fight-or-flight response—kicks into high gear. Adrenaline courses through your veins. Your senses are on high alert. And your anxiety, from first a physiological and then a psychological response, is stimulated.

This is not the same as doing a guided meditation for a short period of time, in a room where you're safe, for a particular purpose. But if you desire to live in that other imaginary world, or in a spiritual state that disconnects you from your body frequently, this is how your body can feel. When you come back into your body and experience what is here, you'll feel the anxiety as a physical nervous system response to the body's feeling, "Where the hell were you? You left me here alone and vulnerable!" You may have left your body to escape your anxiety, but coming back to anxiety that you've avoided feels worse! And this creates a vicious circle of avoiding anxiety, leaving the body, returning to the body, feeling more anxiety... You get the picture.

Being in the Body Feels Safe for the Body

The solution to this dilemma is learning how to be present in the body. The "Presence" and "Embodiment" chapters cover these skills in detail. For now, just know that it is possible to feel safe in your body in the here and now, and that by being in your body, you can develop proficiency at shifting out of the sympathetic nervous system into the parasympathetic—the relaxation response. That is far more effective at calming anxiety than dissociating from the body and abandoning it!

Chapter 6

Spiritual Mistake #4
You Create Your Reality

"As soon as you allow where you are to be all right, you will be able to get where you want to be much faster."

—Bashar/Darryl Anka

This one may surprise you, because the Law of Attraction—the concept that we create our own reality—is extremely popular in spiritual circles and New Thought churches. However, misunderstanding the application of "you create your reality" can be another mistake made by aspirants on the spiritual path that exacerbates fear, worry, and stress.

Don't worry—I'm not going to tell you to stop using the Law of Attraction to manifest what you want in your life. It's a very powerful and effective spiritual tool, used properly. But I want you to take a closer look at it and how you apply it.

What Is the Law of Attraction?

For those of you who may be new to this concept, the Law of Attraction became very popular with the release of the movie *The Secret* and the work of a number of well-known spiritual teachers who were in the movie or associated with it, such as the Abraham/Hicks teachings. In essence, this spiritual principle states that we attract whatever we hold in our consciousness. In other words, our thoughts create our reality.

Olivia Tiffin, author of *The Happiness Textbook: The Ultimate Manual for Mastering Law of Attraction*, describes it this way: "The most simple and basic description of [the] law of attraction is that like attracts like. You attract what you think about. Your thoughts have a frequency, and [the] law of attraction matches the frequency of your thoughts with manifestations of the same frequency."

There is a lot of truth to this practice, and you can experience the results by holding a clear intent in your mind and seeing what happens as a result. For example, if you focus on the idea that people are helpful and kind, and you really believe that thought and feel it in your heart, you're much more likely to experience other people doing kind acts. Some of this result is from what you attract, and a lot of it is from what you choose to put your attention on.

The Law of Anxiety

Unfortunately for many of us, we can use the Law of Attraction to create more anxiety. This is what I call the *Law of Anxiety*: if you worry about what you're thinking, you'll worry *more* about what you're thinking. If you fear what you're thinking, you'll become more afraid of your thoughts. If you're stressed out about the thoughts you have, you'll create more stressed-out thoughts.

Sarah, a highly savvy spiritual person who has studied many modalities of healing and transformation, including yoga, somatics, and energy work, found that the Law of Attraction agitated her anxiety more and more. She described it as a constant spin: "Oh my God. I'm thinking negatively again. I'd spin and spin and spin, worrying that I'm worrying." What she had hoped would calm her by creating the reality she desired simply kept her in the anxiety loop.

The Pride/Shame Polarity

In addition to causing us to constantly monitor our thoughts—and potentially stress out about them—the Law of Attraction, when it is *successful*, can potentially pull us into a tricky kind of polarity. If we manifest something that pleases us, we feel pride. I did that. I'm powerful, special, and maybe spiritually advanced. That very hubris can hinder our spiritual growth by distorting our self-concept into something bigger than we are. It can reinforce the ego's idea of being better than someone else or being important. Then, in order to maintain this inflated sense of self, we have to keep doing it—we have to keep creating more, bigger, and better. There will never be enough, because now, the ego is dependent on a continual performance of attracting desirable things. As the Buddha warned us, desire is the root of suffering.

Sooner or later, we'll be disappointed by something. The attachment to one end of the polarity, the pride pole, begins to attract the polar opposite to balance it out. The side we are avoiding, by clinging to being proud, is shame. Once again, the practice of the Law of Attraction—*under some distorted perceptions of it*—can cause anxiety and pain. This is where the practice of nonattachment is essential when we're working with the Law of Attraction, and I'll explain more about that in Chapter 8.

Case Study: What Did I Do Wrong?

Take the example of Jesstina. A bodyworker and healer, she prided herself on taking good care of her body. She chose organics, avoided sugar, and ate lots of fruits and veggies—all the things that she thought would support her healthy body. She practiced Law of Attraction and believed that if she kept her thoughts positive, she'd always be healthy and strong.

But one day, she felt a lump in her breast, and, before she knew it, she was forced into the world of breast cancer, lumpectomies, and chemotherapy...all her worst nightmares. She felt tremendous shame and despair: "What did I do wrong?" Jesstina lamented over what she believed were her failings with the Law of Attraction, what "wrong" thoughts she must have had, to have allowed this to happen to her body.

It was a struggle not to spiral down into shame and self-judgment at a time when she needed to be kind and loving toward herself. She focused on her healing, and the cancer went into remission. But even years later, she still felt anxiety from that self-blame and wondered if it was all her fault.

It doesn't help to blame yourself when things go wrong, and it doesn't mean that you were bad or had all the wrong thoughts. Although it can be enlightening and healing to recognize ways that we create our suffering, turning it into an all-out attack on ourselves for not being perfect won't change things for the better. It perpetuates the same negative patterns we're trying to transform.

Control Issues

"Creating your reality," albeit an empowering practice when applied with discernment, can trigger other issues lurking beneath the surface—such as the desire to control. It's tempting to look at the Law of Attraction and believe, "Yes, now I know how to control everything! I've got the keys to the kingdom and can make everything work out just right."

But there is a difference between holding the feeling and intent of the experience you would like to have in your consciousness and insisting on things happening in the exact way you envision and at the time you would like. The truth is: the Universe knows better.

Mike Dooley, *New York Times* bestselling author and a known leader of Law of Attraction teachings, reminds us: "Never compromise a dream. Do what you must. The fears, beasts, and mountains before you are part of the plan...don't let your eyes deceive you, for even as you read these words, your ship swiftly approaches."

We want to control what happens, when, and how, but that's not how the Universe rolls. It will respond to your intent, to be sure. However, it doesn't always show up as expected. Sometimes, we meet with obstacles just before our vision manifests—those beasts and mountains Mike Dooley mentioned, which are part of the process.

Control isn't freedom. We believe that it is: that if we could do anything we wanted and make everything happen the way we want, it would erase all our fears. Everything would be nice and predictable and always turn out good. In *Infinite Possibilities*, Dooley says, "Whenever you don't know what lies around the corner, you can choose to be frightened or happy about it, and whichever you choose will affect, influence, and even decide those mysterious moments to come."

We know that life isn't completely predictable. Nor would we want it to be. In fact, it's not just bad things that happen unexpectedly—sometimes, it's the most wonderful, magical, amazing things that happen when they are completely unanticipated. The Divine can manifest your vision in ways that you can't even conceive of right now. Do you really want to shut all that off for the sake of control?

If we look to control everything with the concept of the Law of Attraction, it will only serve to intensify our anxiety. It's great when you feel in command, but the second when something unpredictable and uncomfortable happens, then what?

Life isn't intended to be controlled. All of life is spontaneously arising from Infinite Potential. It is the natural creative urge of the cosmos. That also includes times when we stub our toes, catch the flu, and, yes, someday when we all will die. There is a beautiful Divine plan to all of that, if we allow ourselves to trust it and see it. The purpose of being able to manifest what you wish is for that Divine creativity to flow through you, not for you to become a control freak.

The World Is a Co-Creation

Yes, we can affect many things. You can go out and have fun manifesting parking spaces. You can build an amazing business, attract a loving partner, or heal a physical condition. But there is more to it than what you are doing alone in your manifesting work.

We can't make every day sunny, especially if you live in Michigan or the Amazon rainforest. Nor would you want to change the climate like that. If we had nothing but balmy and sunny days, which might be ideal for you (or rainy, take your pick), the earth would become a crispy planet in fairly short order. We need rain, snow, wind, and thunderstorms. Nature has an intelligence that is beyond our understanding, and it knows what is needed. We can contribute by our choices, but there are uncounted numbers of beings that are creating together here on this planet and in this universe, in a wild and beautiful co-creation.

Yes, there are an awful lot of us out there creating, and we regularly cross paths and bump into each other. You may not like the smog in Los Angeles or Beijing, but you can't just change that reality on your own. A lot of people—including you and I—have contributed to creating that reality. Same with the forests that have been depleted, or the powerful movements over history like the abolition of slavery and standing up for women's rights. These global changes took many people creating a new reality together through both the negative periods of history and the positive.

The Secret about the Secret

So we have an effect on what is happening out there, but creating your reality is more about what is happening in here— inside of you.

Here's a little something that you may have guessed about the Law of Attraction—the secret alluded to in the film of the same name. We don't really create Reality, with a capital R. We create our *experience* of reality, with a small r.

Reality with a capital **R** is the unchanging, infinite Truth. It is the realm of the Infinite Intelligence, beyond form and formlessness, that is the substratum of All That Is. Our lowercase **r**eality is the infinite possible expressions that can arise out of that underlayer.

You are creating that lowercase **r**eality, right in this moment and every moment. But it's not about controlling all that out there and making particular events happen. That may be part of it. But the real magic of the Law of Attraction is transforming *who you are* in *response* to All That Is.

What you always can create, choose, and manifest are your *responses* to what is, your perceptions, and your actions. You have the ability to choose any response to any situation. As a fellow traveler through life, you'll journey through a wide variety of experiences: that's the adventure you signed up for!

The real power of creating your reality is choosing how you will *perceive* what is. Did your candidate lose the election? You can see that with despair and defeat, or you can look at it as a call to action to create the change you'd like to see. Laid up in bed with a nasty cold? Well, you could lament about missing work or feeling miserable, or you could see it as an opportunity to get that much-needed rest, treat yourself with some TLC, and enjoy the book that's been sitting on your nightstand for months.

You create your reality by how you respond. If your response causes you anxiety, don't fret, my dear. You can choose again. You can take the opportunity to embrace yourself with compassion, remember that you don't need to be perfect, and keep practicing.

True freedom comes not from controlling all the events outside you but knowing that you can respond to whatever arises in life. You've got this!

Chapter 7

Spiritual Mistake #5
Feeling the Pain of the World

"All virtues have a shadow."

—Elaine N. Aron

This is a pretty short chapter, because you probably looked at the title and thought, "I know *exactly* what she is talking about!" I introduced this issue in Chapter 2 with Melissa's example of being a Highly Sensitive Person, and I have also written a couple chapters in the Spiritual Keys section (the "Embodiment" and "Self-Compassion" chapters) that address the problems arising from this tendency. But it is worth identifying here as a spiritual mistake that creates more worry and increases our suffering.

I get it. As spiritual folks, we deeply care about others, whether human or not. We hear of the suffering of children with AIDS in Africa, dwindling dolphin, rhino, and gorilla populations, rainforest devastation, earthquakes in the Pacific rim, and the war-torn Middle East. I could go on, but that's probably more than enough to evoke a worried look on your face and anxiety beginning to build.

But feeling the pain of the world doesn't serve anyone. While it is important to have compassion and empathy, it's also important to protect ourselves from *compassion fatigue*, which can cause physical, mental, and emotional injury. According to the Compassion Fatigue Awareness Project (www. compassionfatigue.org), compassion fatigue is "an extreme state

of tension and preoccupation with the suffering of those being
helped to the degree that it can create a secondary traumatic
stress for the helper." As folks who put high value on the qualities
of compassion and service to those in need, we also need to be
mindful of how we go about those acts of kindness. If we allow
ourselves to become overwhelmed by the suffering of others, we
won't be able to effectively serve our purpose in the world, and it
can hinder our own spiritual awakening.

Natural Empaths

The majority of those of us on the spiritual path are natural-
born *empaths*—another term similar to HSPs (Highly Sensitive
Persons). We have finely attuned radar. We can pick up on what
others are feeling, and we can also easily put ourselves in the
place of another who is suffering. As a result, watching, reading,
or listening to the news can be an exercise in anxiety, fear, and
being overwhelmed. Our hearts go out to every suffering human,
animal, and plant, and the whole world can feel like one big
painful wound.

For those of us who are empaths, the unconscious tendency is to
run the pain of the world through our own nervous system. We
might even believe that it is the "more spiritual" thing to do: to
deeply understand and connect with others in pain. We believe
we can handle it, and we think it's the right thing to do. Then we
wonder why we feel fried and freaked out.

Compassion, not Confusion

There's a difference, however, between feeling compassion for the suffering of others and confusing it with creating our own suffering. If we wear ourselves down or even make ourselves ill by taking on collective pain, is that really spiritual? Are we truly helping anyone? Is it bringing us more inner peace—or increasing our anxiety? Robin Stern, associate director of the Yale Center for Emotional Intelligence, asserted in an article in the *Washington Post* ("Being Empathetic Is Good, but It Can Hurt Your Health") that those who regularly prioritize others' emotions over their own are more susceptible to experiencing anxiety or low-level depression.

Let's not confuse service to others and the planet with absorbing all the negative energy around us in an effort to care, understand, or help out. All that does is increase our feeling of overwhelm and despair. Let's also be mindful not to confuse the emotions of others with our own. When we take on the pain of the world, we may be unconsciously processing emotions that don't belong to us through our own physical and energetic bodies. This causes us unnecessary suffering and can even create physical problems like illness or chronic fatigue.

Compassion allows us to recognize someone else's pain, attempt to understand it, and express our caring in some helpful way. It doesn't mean that we must put ourselves through exactly what that person or animal is feeling. As a spiritual practice, compassion should empower us to take helpful action to alleviate the pain—and for that, we need to feel strong, centered, and calm within.

Respond Rather Than React

When we take on the pain of others, we're reacting rather than responding. We are feeling the emotions as if they are our own, and, in that way, allowing them to trigger our own issues in addition to the suffering we see around us. This is reactivity, not higher consciousness.

In order to respond rather than react, we need to be aware of what happens in us when we're exposed to an upsetting situation. We have a number of thoughts that might arise, like "How terrible! Something must be done! I can't stand this. I have to do something now. It will be horrible if it isn't stopped." Naturally, this brings on fear.

The compassion we feel transforms into fear of what is happening, which triggers our anxiety and the fight/flight/ freeze/faint response within us. It can incapacitate us (freeze or faint), cause us to withdraw (flight), or create an overreaction that may attack the problem in an unhelpful way (fight). Now, this becomes *our* issue of fear, rather than focusing on what is helpful to the situation.

Notice if you have an anxiety reaction to someone's pain, whether to a close friend or an animal you saw on a YouTube video. Ask yourself if your reaction is helpful to the situation. What would be the most helpful response if you weren't triggered into anxiety?

True compassion (known as *karuna* in Sanskrit, pronounced like car-oo-NUH) is deep and complex, and it includes looking at the source of suffering within all of us. While considering how to be of help to others in the situation, also take a look at how you can find the source of your own suffering with this issue within yourself. Is there a belief that these situations shouldn't exist?

Is there blame of someone or something that makes you feel powerless and fearful? Do you unconsciously believe that if you don't do something immediately, everything will get worse?

Karuna and Upeksha

Karuna, the practice of compassion in yogic philosophy, is said to maintain serenity of mind when faced with others who suffer. But you won't be able to access that serenity if you use compassion to create fear, worry, and overwhelm in yourself.

Additionally, compassion shouldn't disempower either the one who suffers or you. See the situation as one that can be healed or transformed. Trust that your response matters, even if it doesn't "fix" it completely. Let whatever you can offer be enough. And don't create more suffering in the world by taking it all on energetically and emotionally and then feeling like you will fall apart. That doesn't help anyone.

The practice of *upeksha*, even-mindedness (which we explored in Chapter 4), can assist in being compassionate from a more centered, calm, and courageous place. When we see suffering, especially a global situation like human trafficking, for example, there is also a judgment. This is wrong, the people who perpetuate this are horrible, etc. We may even be right about that. But if we buy into those thoughts, it can take us into an anxiety reaction, and we may become less effective in creating the change in order to "right those wrongs" and end the painful cycle. We do *not* need anxiety as the motivator and juice to impel us to take right action.

Clarity and Empowerment

Try to notice the situation from the even-minded clarity of
upeksha: "it's true, this is causing harm to others, and I want to
make a difference. I feel called to some sort of action." From a
deeply caring place within us, we see what can be done without
attacking those we see as perpetrators. *Upeksha* helps us to
shift out of attacking those who have done the harm to healing
and empowering those who are suffering. We can find our own
empowerment within as well by not allowing this situation to
perpetuate more suffering by amplifying it within ourselves.

Explore your thoughts, beliefs, and reactions on a deeper level
to help shift yourself out of an anxiety reaction to the pain of the
world. You don't need to take it on as your own. Having healthy
energetic boundaries is also tremendously helpful when noticing
pain and suffering on the planet. In Part III, I will give you the
tools to be more compassionate toward yourself in the process
and to create and sustain those energetic boundaries.

For now, we'll move on to the last of the six spiritual mis-takes .

Chapter 8

Spiritual Mistake #6
The Safety/Danger Polarity

"The wise man in the storm prays not for safety from danger, but deliverance from fear."

—Ralph Waldo Emerson

The last mistake that I see spiritual folks typically make (although there may be others— email me at Connie@ AwakeningSelf.com if you have another one!) is what I call the Safety/Danger polarity.

I've already talked about the Pride/Shame polarity, and I'll back up just a bit to talk about polarities, because they are all around us in this three-dimensional world in which we live. It's part and parcel of human existence to experience polarities. There's hot and cold, up and down, tight and loose—you get the picture. Everything on the planet and everything you experience within you has its opposite.

But on the spiritual path, we can learn to transcend them. The ability to transcend polarities goes a long way toward reducing our anxiety and stress. In *The Marriage of Spirit*, unity consciousness teachers Leslie Temple-Thurston and Brad Laughlin reveal this practice. "It is possible to find the underlying unity inherent in all the pairs of opposites within us. Finding this unity is an awakening to a more expanded state of consciousness and to our spiritual essence." Transcendence happens in this unity consciousness.

What Is Safety? What Is Danger?

In order to transcend a polarity, we first need to pull it apart in order to understand what is operating within those opposite forces. Let's look at safety first.

Safety is the condition of being safe from undergoing or causing any harm, injury, or loss. Danger is right there in the concept of safety. You really can't think about one without the other. When we feel in danger, we want to be safe. When we're safe, we're avoiding danger. We do everything in our power to feel safe and to protect our loved ones from danger. It's the most fundamental instinct we have. If we aren't safe, we're not as likely to survive.

The idea of safety brings us right back to the desire for control. If things are in our control, then we're going to feel safe, right? We like what is known and in our control, and consciously or unconsciously, we spend a lot of our energy every day trying to feel safe.

You may not think that we're so invested in creating safety, because most of us aren't running away from wild tigers anymore. But the bigger challenge in Western culture these days is our *psyche* feeling safe. There are all kinds of threats to our emotional well-being and sense of ourselves. Do they or don't they like me? Will they accept or reject my proposal? Am I a good parent or a bad parent, and are others judging my parenting? Will I be perceived as successful or a failure? All of these scenarios cause that fear factor to be activated when we are basing our sense of safety in the world—and our sense of self—on things, circumstances, and people outside of us.

Danger is, naturally, the possibility of being hurt or injured. Our sense of danger is relative to how we perceive things. If we perceive threats all around us, whether physical, mental, emotional, or spiritual, our anxiety is going to be high.

We often associate danger with the unknown and chaos. When things are out of our control, our spidey-senses inside can be habituated to perceiving danger, like how it feels when we're walking around in the dark at night. The dark obscures our vision, so we really can't tell what is out there; it's unknown. Fear is often projected on the unknown, going all the way back to our cave(wo)man days when we had to be on high alert at nighttime and carry a big, preferably flaming, stick.

It Shouldn't Be Like This

There's a subtle attitude we have when we're clinging to the idea of safety. We believe that it shouldn't be like this—it shouldn't be unpredictable and unknown. It shouldn't be "dangerous." It shouldn't be chaotic.

When things change, we tend to feel anxious, like it's not safe anymore if it isn't familiar. If we didn't win, that's bad and our sense of self can feel endangered: "Oh no, am I a loser? They're asking me to speak in front of the class—I'm not prepared, that's so scary! I shouldn't have to do that, things shouldn't change, I shouldn't ever lose." There are so many ways in which we psychologically perceive danger, which increases our anxiety.

But there is no "should" or "shouldn't" in life. Our shoulds exist in our mind alone; life simply *is*. There's no document that says life should always be safe. And honestly, there's nothing that says that life is always dangerous.

We Make It Bigger by Pushing It Away

We have explored how resisting and pushing away makes things stay. It also gives what you resist power and makes it bigger than it really is. When we perceive something with fear, believe that it is dangerous, and then try to get rid of it, it looks really huge.

Take a spider, for example. I used to have a big fear of spiders. Growing up, I'd go screaming to my dad when I found one in my bathroom, which is usually where they would lurk. Even well into my adulthood, I had this crazy fear of spiders.

One time, I locked myself out of my house. I lived in a studio apartment that was on the second floor of an old, early twentieth century farmhouse. The only way I could get back in was to crawl around on the roof of the first floor to the window next to my bed and crack the window open. I knew it wasn't locked, because it was very difficult for me to turn the rusty lock and the window itself was very hard to pry open.

With a lot of huffs and puffs, I finally got the bottom window frame to slide up, allowing me enough space to slide myself in. But as I looked down, there was my big fear, looking up at me with its hairy brown legs and beady eyes (which of course I couldn't see, but I knew were there)—a spider. It was probably about an inch from toe to toe (do spiders have toes?), not very big. But to me, it seemed big, hairy, and ready to bite me. Potentially poisonous? Not likely, but still, you never know.

What was I to do? I'd have to crawl right over it. It had conveniently placed itself right there on the edge of the sill, as if laughing at me—*you'll never cross this threshold while I'm here!* I had to figure out to what to do. So I took my shoe, raised it slowly, slammed it down—and missed. The spider went into my bed.

Oh @%#*! That was the last thing I wanted. *Now it's somewhere in my bed, and I'll have to find it. What if I don't, and I go to bed, and it comes out in the middle of the night and jumps on me! It could bite me all over. I'd never be able to sleep.* My anxiety was through the roof, and this spider was now ruling my world.

The short story here (which is already plenty long!) is that I spent the next twenty minutes ripping apart my bed, jumping all over the mattress whacking at the spider with my shoe, and screaming bloody murder. I wonder what my neighbors thought was going on.

After that, I made a decision. This was stupid. OK, I'm not going to judge myself, but this was really silly. I know intellectually that a spider is not a big deal and isn't really going to harm me unless it's poisonous, and I knew this one wasn't. It was just an ordinary spider. But I made it sooooo big with my fear, with my perception that all spiders are dangerous.

So I worked on my fear over the years, and now I see spiders as regular creatures who help keep the fly population down, and I have an effective technique of catching them in a plastic cup and taking them outside to the bushes, where they belong (according to me!). Hence, my daughter doesn't have a fear of spiders, either. I shifted my perception away from believing spiders were big and dangerous and brought it back down to reality.

Being Spiritual Makes Me Safe, Right?

You may be wondering why the Safety/Danger polarity is a spiritual mistake, because all of these situations are part of anyone's life. The interesting thing is that some of us pursue the spiritual path in part because we think it will make us safe.

If I chant mantras, I'll be protected. By visualizing my shield of energy around me, it will repel any negativity. If I just meditate more, I'll be so calm and peaceful that I'll never feel fear again. All of these examples show the subtle way that we use our spiritual practices to create an illusion of safety.

Oh no, you say! Do you mean those things aren't protecting me? They could be. But nothing is foolproof. They may be helping you to *feel* more safe. But that isn't really the point.

The Illusion of Safety/Danger

If we look deeply at the spiritual aspects of this polarity, we see that the ideas of safety and danger are both our creation. There is no absolutely safe situation, nor is there an inherently dangerous one. Handling a cobra would be a very poor choice for me and probably for you as well, but a skilled snake charmer does it every day for a living. Safety and Danger are illusory concepts.

Life is neither safe nor dangerous. It just is what it is, in every moment. It is true that we can make choices that put us in more safe situations or dangerous ones. But when we buy into the idea that we *must* feel safe (according to our perceptions of what is dangerous), try to control things (whether spiritually or practically) to avoid danger, and then freak out when things don't go as planned, it simply perpetuates the anxiety we're trying to release.

There are other possibilities of experience besides safety or danger. When we are present in the moment, we can step out of controlling and away from the mind's interpretation of things and learn to be with how they actually are. Living in the present moment helps us transcend our fears of what will happen and stay right with the reality of how it is *right now*.

There are many other perspectives we can embrace that shift us out of the Safety/Danger polarity which have nothing to do with changing what's "out there," yet allow us to see it differently. Taking my spider story, we can perceive the Oneness of all things and see ourselves in the spider. We can choose to accept the spider and the situation and wait for a resolution to reveal itself. The spider can be welcomed in (but you don't have to get too close, wink wink) as part of the wholeness of the world and even as some part of your own self. And by surrendering and placing our trust in the Divine ("Surrender" chapter coming up!), we can allow something greater than us to bring forth our highest good. Doesn't that potentially sound like a wonderful, calming spiritual practice? Transcending the polarity of Safety/Danger and taking responsibility for changing our own perception gives us true freedom to be able to handle whatever life brings.

Now, I'm going to show you the steps to get there—to resolve these spiritual mis-takes and the other anxiety triggers in your life. With these building-block practices, you'll be able to create more and more ease in your life and slowly allow that pesky anxiety to dissolve away.

Chapter 9

How You Do Spirituality Is How You Do Everything

*"Spiritual practice is not just sitting and meditation...
Every act, every breath, and every step can be practice
and can help us to become more ourselves."*

—Thich Nhat Hahn

We often like to think of our spiritual path as something separate, something outside of everything else we do. Or at least we think of the practices that way. I sit to meditate, and then I balance my checkbook. This morning, I'm going to chant for fifteen minutes and then head off to work. We act as if what we cultivate in our spiritual practices is separate from our lives.

If you've been on the path for a while, you know that spirituality is about *living* it, not just practicing it. Yet there's also another level to this that we overlook.

It's not just *what* we choose to do when we strive for our spiritual awakening—it's *how* we do it. The old adage holds true: "How you do anything is how you do everything." Specifically, in this case, *how* you do your spiritual practices reflects your attitude, beliefs, and approach to most other things in life. Another way to say this is that what happens in how you practice is a microcosm for the rest of your life—and especially for how and why your anxiety shows up.

So when I'm teaching a yoga class, for example, I'm not just talking about how to do downward-facing dog pose, i.e., put your hands a little wider than shoulder width apart. Spread your

fingers mindfully, and root the base of each finger as well as the
pads...and so on. I also help the students explore *how* they apply
the actions, both on and off the mat.

Abhyasa and Vairagya

This brings in many different aspects of yoga philosophy, which
I will touch on throughout this book, as well as other universal
spiritual principles. But let's start with the foundational concepts
behind yoga practice: *abhyasa* (pronounced "ub"—as in "tub"—
YAH-suh) and *vairagya* (like vye-RAHG-yuh).

As a side note, I'm going to introduce you to some Sanskrit words
in the process. Some of you will recognize them, and for others
they will be very new and foreign. I love the use of Sanskrit
because it gives us a whole new vocabulary for some of these
ideas. Sanskrit words aren't likely to have other associations you
may have with similar concepts in English, so they can be used
specifically for your spiritual growth. But if they throw you off
a bit, don't worry about it and just use the English translation
instead. You don't need to add Sanskrit anxiety to your list of
anxiety triggers!

OK, back to *abhyasa* and *vairagya*. Georg Feuerstein, author
of *The Yoga Sutras of Patanjali*, asserts that these principles
are "the two poles of any form of yogic discipline." They actually
apply to any spiritual practice you might undertake, such as the
chanting of the rosary in Catholic tradition, being a cantor in a
synagogue, or any kind of meditation.

What Does *Practice* Really Mean?

Let's begin with *abhyasa*, which literally means, "practice." You might be thinking, OK, we know practice is important. But do we really?

Because the truth is that many of us spiritual folks forget that we're practicing. We believe that we're *perfecting*. In fact, spiritually oriented people, perhaps more than the average person, may be more inclined to be perfectionists, as we noted in the chapter on perfectionism. We expect to do it "right," and we work oh-so-hard to get there. We don't even realize that it's about the journey, not the destination.

Before we go into the details of what practice truly means, I want to acknowledge that most of us don't need to be reminded of the fact that we should practice. We already know what to do! We don't need to be told to do it more or that we need to try harder. That just increases our anxiety, because we're probably already beating ourselves up over that. The thing that we need to remember is that it is *practice*. You're going to be imperfect. Mistakes will be made, and you'll sometimes fall off the horse and have to get back up on it again. You may forget to meditate for a day, a month, even a year. That's OK—please be kind to yourself as you practice *imperfectly*!

Abhyasa—practice—is all about the journey, and so is spirituality. There is no set endpoint, and honestly, would we really want that? You may be convinced right now that "Yes, I want an endpoint to this, to get to the ultimate goal (both enlightenment and the end of my anxiety!)." But often, that desire is fueled by an aversion within us—an aversion to how it is. We want to get to that perfect ending so that we don't have to

do this anymore. We won't have to suffer, we wouldn't have to
deal with problems, we won't have fluctuations of emotions, we
won't have to be faced with frustrating relationships.

Hmmm, sounds more like a computer program than a human.
Bots, anyone?

I don't think you want to become a robot, and I certainly don't.
We came here to live life and experience being human—to
be spiritual beings having a human experience. We want
to experience aliveness, joyfulness, and success, as well as
challenges. And that includes the experience of challenging
emotions like anxiety. Through practice, we learn to deal with
those emotions more consciously and gracefully.

The Aspects of Practice

Life is really about practice. It's about learning new things each
day. And most certainly, spiritual life is a process of opening up
to a more expansive, profound, loving, and empowered way of
being. That doesn't come about via a bolt of lightning (at least
not for 99.999 percent of us). It happens from being willing to sit
on the cushion to meditate again and again, to roll out the yoga
mat, to open our hearts to those who are suffering, or to make
the time to connect to the Divine in sincere prayer, for example.

That's the first aspect of practice—to practice *consistently*. It's
not just a spiritual truth; athletes know this, too. In fact, athletes
know that there's no end to the process of being an athlete, not
until you're ready to retire. Even after winning the hundred-yard
dash at the Olympics, sprinters like Usain Bolt are looking at
how they can beat that time. They're always striving to see what

is possible next. And so they practice repeatedly, they learn, and they explore the next possibility.

The other aspects of practice, according to yoga philosophy, are practicing *over a long period of time,* and practicing *with devotion.* So if you've been on this path for some time, you know that we're looking at the long haul here. In the beginning, we hope for rapid transformation. We might even receive it. But then we're there and realize, wow, there's so much more. Sticking with the plan and continuing to practice, day after day, year after year, is essential to experiencing transformation. Then there is devotion. If we aren't putting our hearts into what we're doing—on the mat or off—then we won't reap many benefits from the practice.

We have a spiritual paradox here, and it is one that applies to our anxiety. I've already reminded you not to beat yourself up over your practice. At the same time, I'm asserting that you'll need to practice (whether you engage in a spiritual practice or use the principles in this book to overcome your anxiety) consistently, over a long period of time, with devotion. On the path to awakening, we learn to embrace the paradox. We can be compassionate toward ourselves about the challenges of practicing and doing it imperfectly at the same time that we encourage ourselves to keep coming back to the work, over and over again.

It is possible to motivate yourself and keep practicing without being harsh on yourself. You don't need to turn spirituality into something anxiety-provoking. The tools in this book will allow you to simultaneously calm your anxiety as well as spiritually evolve. You can come back into your heart, connect with yourself, and remember what really matters to you. Your spiritual growth matters, and healing your anxiety matters. Then sit back down on the meditation cushion again, even if you're in a bad mood

or think it sucks. Or take a nap, give yourself a break, and come
back to it with a self-compassionate heart. The truth is that it's
all practice, whether or not you're on the meditation cushion,
when you're approaching life with awareness and the intent
to grow, awaken, and heal. This circles us back to the *how* of
spiritual growth.

Not the What, But the How

I'll use another yoga analogy here, because I see this often with
my students. We'll be doing a pose like triangle pose, and I'll
ask them, what are you experiencing? What are you feeling?
And very importantly, what are you thinking? Initially, a yoga
practitioner is mainly focused on the "getting it right" aspect:
are my feet positioned properly? Am I feeling the opening in
my hamstring and inner thigh? Have I aligned my spine, and is
my weight distributed properly? Then, they may start to take a
look at their breath. How am I breathing? Am I still doing Ujjayi
breath? Are my breaths deep or shallow? You get the idea.

Here is where the practice—and again, this is with any spiritual
practice you might undertake—gets more interesting, profound,
and where the deeper spiritual transformation occurs. It's when
we begin to notice thoughts and emotions. Many times, a student
has started sobbing in child's pose because they are finally aware
of a flood of emotion, or a train of thought surfaces that has been
unconscious until that moment.

How are you thinking about the practice? Are you constantly
comparing yourself to others, or to some ideal of how you
should be? For example, it's common for meditators—even
longtime meditators—to get frustrated because they can't
seem to quiet their thoughts down. It's probably the number

one frustration that spiritual people express to me. There's a belief, an expectation, that they *should* be able to turn off the volume on thinking, and that they're failing if they aren't doing that. They believe that they must sit still or else they're a poor meditator. They expect to be able to control the process, especially controlling the body and the thoughts. The critic looms large; they look around and see all these still, peaceful looking people, and they think, "The others have it, and I don't." A flood of shame and hopelessness comes over them, and with it a wave of anxiety. They may have thoughts like, "I'm not good enough," "I'm not doing it right," "I'm incapable," and so on.

Then, another level of *how* you practice may come to your attention. The anxiety about keeping up with others, about being good enough, and about trying to get it perfect might cause you to force things upon yourself. Going farther into a pose than your body is ready for, insisting you sit through pain in your knees when you've injured them recently, or jumping headlong into new poses or practices without proper preparation is setting yourself up to fail. Let alone loading yourself down with worries about what other people will think; this is how we *perceive* our practice, which is often through comparison.

On the other side of the coin, your beliefs and attitudes about yourself may hold you back. You might give up on a pose, a martial arts move, or a daily practice of gratitude because you believe you can't do it. The anxiety about not being strong enough, consistent enough, or as good as the person next to you—or feeling that it's just too difficult and uncomfortable—can keep you from exploring and growing past your edge. You stay stuck in the same pattern and the same way of living your life and hinder your personal and spiritual growth.

Doing Violence to Ourselves

We may end up doing violence to ourselves in how we practice. This could be physical—you can certainly get injured doing yoga, ecstatic dance, martial arts, or even sitting meditation. But the greater harm is usually the mental and emotional violence we do to ourselves in how we think about the way we're practicing and what we believe about ourselves. And this shows up in class, in sangha, in church, and out in the world.

Besides being self-critical, we end up doing violence to ourselves by trying to push away aspects of our lives or the challenges that arise on the spiritual path. We want to make the discomfort, the fear, the tension, the nervousness all go away. We resist the thoughts and emotions that arise, and we wish that we could simply get rid of the anxiety.

This actually does more harm than good. Certainly, we want to change our habits and the way we approach spirituality and our lives so that anxiety is unlikely to arise. But if we try to push it away, it will stay; as they say, "What you resist, persists." Not only will the anxiety continue to boil beneath the surface when we try to repress it, but the attempt to simply "get rid" of something within us is an act of violence. We are cutting ourselves up into pieces we like and pieces we don't like.

There's a more compassionate, healing, and transformative way to grow and evolve. It's not about being perfect, and you don't need to get rid of anything. We forget that it's all—every aspect of spirituality as well as your life—*practice*. The true intent is to be showing up and giving it a go, every day; to see what is possible in this moment, in our bodies, hearts, and spirits; and to let ourselves make mis-takes and let go of perfection.

The Second Principle—Vairagya

If we practice with perfectionism and the need to control, we see how that sets up a dynamic that causes us to feel disappointment and anxiety. So it's essential that we bring in the other end of the two "poles" of yoga philosophy: *vairagya*. It assists us in practicing without creating anxiety about it.

Vairagya is translated as "nonattachment" or "dispassion." In the *Bhagavad Gita*, one of the great spiritual texts of Hinduism, we are encouraged to be "unattached to the fruits of our labors." This is an example of the practice of *vairagya*. This means practicing just for practice's sake.

When we practice with attachment to outcome, we feed the ego: the aspect of our personality that attempts to control everything and needs to feel important. Either we do well, which pleases our ego and reinforces the desire to control everything (therefore reinforcing one of the main roots of anxiety), or we don't do so well, and the ego steps in and says, "I should control you even more, so we will perform better and won't be so disappointed next time." Believing that thought only pulls you further into the vicious cycle.

We cannot find calm and ease within if we are constantly seeking after certain results. Yes, set goals and work toward them, but do that without needing to experience those goals in a rigid form or time.

If you want to be able to sit for forty-five minutes of meditation (or want to return to a level of meditation you had before), you'll probably be more successful if you appreciate being able to sit for five minutes to start. If you're singing a devotional song, allow for the fluctuations of your pitch and range, and if you're praying and can't tap into the heartfelt feeling, then acknowledge yourself

for the intent to feel a connection to God, even if you didn't
notice it today. Go easy on yourself, but don't give up. *Vairagya*,
or nonattachment, doesn't suggest that you just sit back and
relax, but rather continue to practice with open-mindedness and
appreciation for whatever is.

The Inner Witness

The practice of *vairagya* cultivates what is known as the *inner
witness*, or the neutral or detached observer. It is a part of our
selves—our consciousness—that can step back and observe what
happens without being involved in the situation. We all have
that part of ourselves. Many spiritual traditions consider this to
be our true essence, that which is beyond thought, emotion, or
sensation. It simply *is,* and it is capable of being present with and
aware of everything without narration or judgment.

Vairagya, nonattachment, helps us develop our inner witness
self (or more accurately, helps us become more attuned to the
fact that it is there and utilize it). We will need that inner witness
to be online and active in order to shift ourselves out of the
misperceptions of perfectionism, judgment, fear, doubt, and
other feelings that cause our anxiety in the first place.

The Paradox of Awareness

So, we begin to put together the principles of *abhyasa* (practice)
and *vairagya* (nonattachment) in our spiritual endeavors and in
our lives. We become more aware of how we're doing everything.
Am I allowing myself to let go and be a beginner again in this
moment—to simply practice? How can I shift from a hurtful way

of going about my day or my yoga class into a kind, encouraging, accepting approach? We become much more aware of the *what* and the *how*, which leads us to some of the *why* about our anxiety. We begin to understand in new ways why anxiety arises so strongly for us, and we begin to release it.

The paradox of this (yep, another spiritual paradox!) is that, at first, you may find that your anxiety *increases*. Hey, I didn't sign up for that! But be prepared, because it might happen. Don't worry, it's a temporary phase. There are a couple reasons why you may experience more anxiety at first.

Aware of Being Aware

One reason you may be experiencing more anxiety from greater awareness comes back to *how* you are being aware of yourself. You may have increased your awareness, but that sly inner critic slipped through the cracks. The inner critic—the habit of judging and comparing yourself—may be entering into the observations and laying down judgments about how you're practicing or how well you're doing at being nonattached.

You may be attempting to be more detached, but the inner critic says that's not enough. Then, you notice that you've fallen into unconsciousness and left your body, spacing out and tripping off the curb. Bam! The inner critic then lays down another zinger, saying, "See, you're not doing this right. You became unconscious!" On top of that, the slick little critic may then judge you for noticing that you're judging your judgments! You just can't win—until you are willing to let the story go.

When you find yourself in this vicious circle, pause and practice more nonattachment. It's OK if you aren't doing it perfectly. It's

OK that you notice some habits which have caused you suffering, or if you discovered that you're judging yourself. You are OK. There's nothing wrong with you. Take a deep breath and hold yourself with compassion. I'm going to walk you through how to do that in the "Self-Compassion" chapter.

You're Noticing What Is Already There

Why else might your anxiety be exacerbated? Because you're becoming more aware of what you do that causes the anxiety, and you're noticing the worry, fear, and stress more. It's a misperception that the anxiety increases, in this case—it's simply that you're noticing the lurking anxiety in an overt way now. It can't hide in your unconscious awareness like it used to. You can't pretend not to recognize that it's rearing its head. And so it may seem like you are feeling more anxiety, when you're actually becoming more aware of the fears and worries you have.

Great, you think *that sucks!* But it's a necessary and powerful part of the process. Because once you become aware of something, it's not going to have the same power over you. Awareness means that *you now have a choice*. Before, you were just reacting, just going about life unconsciously and doing what you usually do and getting the results you usually experience from doing that.

Now, you'll notice: "*Hey, I'm feeling kind of stressed out in this forward bend.* I see—it's because I'm comparing myself to that woman who used to come to class who could lay her torso flat over her legs, and I think I should be able to do that." You're noticing that you feel less-than, and you feel your anxiety rise.

At that moment, you can ask yourself: *"Hmm, is that woman here? Does she matter to me? Is this helping me in this pose, in this moment?"* And my favorite question to ask myself when I'm expecting more out of a yoga pose than what I believe I'm getting—is my enlightenment *dependent* on lying flat over my legs in the seated forward bend?

I usually get a good laugh out of that question, because clearly my spiritual awakening (and yours) is *not* dependent on that! I can typically think of a number of other things that might be hindering me, but that forward bend is certainly not one of them! But the way I think about it, the way I perceive and compare myself, the way I make myself feel bad about what I'm experiencing—*those* might be some of the things hindering me.

In that moment, you can begin to use some of the tools we'll explore in Part III to help shift you out of the state of anxiety into new states of well-being.

The Bell Curve of Awareness

As you practice with nonattachment (*abhyasa* and *vairagya*), you will develop expanded awareness. As on a bell curve in a grading chart, there isn't a lot of anxiety at the low end of awareness. This isn't necessarily because it doesn't exist; it's because you're not noticing it. At the top of the curve, you have increased awareness, and so you're noticing the anxiety but not yet able to make a full shift out of it. You're still learning what to practice to do that.

But on the right side of the bell curve—the "A" students—the curve goes down. The anxiety will begin to decrease as awareness increases and expands more fully. You'll catch things faster because your awareness will be keen, and you'll implement changes responsively. Try not to strive for the "A" side of the curve; rather, trust that as you continue with your practices with nonattachment, you'll gradually move in that direction as a natural progression. And by the way, let go of the grading system—no one is grading you on your awakening except you!

An Attitude to Begin With

As you embark on this new path to working with your anxiety, I invite you to explore a spiritual attitude from yoga philosophy. It's called *maitri* (pronounced like MY-tree), and it means friendliness.

You're probably a friendly sort of person—to others. But if you're feeling anxiety and you relate to some of what I've been describing about how you go about your spirituality and your life, you may not be so friendly to yourself.

Think about what a good friend is like. Consider their qualities and how it feels to be around them. You know you're accepted, appreciated, and safe in their company. You know they'll give you encouragement when you're down and listen compassionately when you've blown it. They'll help you feel capable of getting back up on the horse again when you've fallen.

This is the attitude to cultivate toward yourself. Be your own best friend. I know, you've heard it before, but now I really want you to think about how you would treat yourself as a dearly loved friend. When you feel anxious, whatever the cause, *be there* for yourself. This is the essence of *maitri* when applied to ourselves. Like a dear friend, hold yourself in acceptance and love, and remind yourself that, even if this moment is tough, it's not going to last forever.

Part III

The Keys to a More Calm, Confident Life

Now, we will embark on the work of releasing the anxiety. Of course, this is easier said than done. But at the same time, it doesn't have to be difficult or complicated, either.

There are many ways to approach healing anxiety and finding calm within. These keys are a synthesis of what I have found most helpful for myself, my clients, and my students over the years. You may find them a bit novel, although some you may find familiar.

This approach is spiritual and holistic. It incorporates the body as well as the heart, mind, and spirit. It is a comprehensive approach, and each key builds upon the last. So my suggestion is to follow them in sequence and watch how your skills in handling anxiety grow and the fears begin to soften as you move along. The idea is that you'll become more stable, calm, and centered. As these practices empower you, the anxiety will lose its grip on your life.

In the next chapter, I will share with you the first key to transforming your anxiety—and it is all about *being here*.

Chapter 10

Presence

"To be present is to awaken into that dimension of yourself and your life that transcends the thinking mind."

—Leonard Jacobson, *Journey Into Now*

Anxiety is, in essence, an experience of taking ourselves out of the present. Most of us who experience anxiety are not living in the here and now. We are worried about the future or freaking out about something that has already happened...and how that will impact us again in the future. Anxiety is anticipating the worst while ignoring not only the best, but simply whatever *is*.

I haven't yet found someone who has anxiety who isn't doing this. For example, you may have a fear of rattlesnakes. Let's say you live in a location like the foothills of California, where you have a real possibility of coming across them.

You could allow your fear to stop you from enjoying nature because you're anticipating the possibility that a rattlesnake could jump out and bite you. This could cause a lot of agitation and worry. But, in this moment, is that actually a problem? Unless a rattlesnake is actually biting you, which isn't likely in this moment because you're reading this book, then the anxiety is about something that *may* happen or something that did happen in the past and that you fear may happen again.

This isn't to say that what you feel isn't a real emotion, a true concern, and something that you should be mindful of when you're hiking. It's simply that the anxiety itself usually has its source in something other than *right now*. There are other factors that contribute to anxiety, but being present (or in this case, not being so present) is a huge aspect.

What Is Presence?

Presence is simple. It's being right here, right now, with your awareness and attention, with a quiet mind and an open heart. This means that the mind is not telling a story about what is happening, what already happened, or what will happen next. The mind is either silent (which I know may seem impossible right now, so don't worry), or the volume is turned way down, and your attention is on the *now*. When we're fully engaged with what is right here in front of us in this moment, the thoughts are irrelevant and can't coexist with presence.

However, even though presence is incredibly simple, as we have often discovered on the spiritual path, maintaining it isn't necessarily easy. Sometimes, something is so simple that it's right under our nose and completely obvious, but we don't see it because we have a habit of attention that is focused on other things.

Missing What Is in Front of Me

Perhaps this scenario is a bit familiar to you. A couple weeks ago, I was walking around the house looking for my scissors. I really needed them for something, and I knew that they were around in the kitchen. I have a particular place I always put them—up on the windowsill, above the sink. I kept returning to that spot over and over, looking for them there as if maybe the next time, they'd just magically appear where they were "supposed" to be.

After several minutes of frustration, I sat down and let go. I thought maybe I should just go into my daughter's drawers and find a pair of hers. But I stopped for a bit and just sat. And then I saw them—on the countertop next to me, right in plain sight.

In that moment, when I found the scissors, I finally became present. I let go of my stories about where the scissors usually are, that they *should* be there, that I didn't know what I'd do if I didn't find them, getting angry at whoever had moved them (which certainly would *not* have been me!), how this was wasting my time—and finally just sat down and started being present. When I came into the moment with the table, the kitchen countertop, my feet on the hardwood floor, and my shallow breath, I began to look around and see what was actually there. I became present, and that's when I actually perceived what was in front of me the whole time.

A Connection with What Is

Presence is a deep connection with *what is*. The mind is quiet and the heart is open. All of your attention is right on what is in front of you or within you. When we're present with another person, we're listening, we are quiet within, and we feel a bond—a sense of Oneness. Anxiety can't take hold when we feel connection and Oneness.

In fact, it is usually a sense of disconnection—from the world, from Source, from another, and/or from our sense of self—that gives birth to anxiety. Presence is an essential component to transform that disconnection into unity.

How Presence Calms Anxiety

Presence calms anxiety through creating an experience of connection. But how does presence do that?

By turning our attention away from thinking and toward *what is*, we turn the volume down on thoughts: the perpetrators of anxiety. Our thoughts stir up emotional reactions, which in turn stimulate the sympathetic nervous system: the source of our fight-or-flight response (I associate **s**ympathetic with the letter **s** and the word **s**tress to remember the effect stress has on the nervous system). Agitating thoughts create stress, worry, and fear and kick in the feeling that we are not safe and need to be on guard lest something come after us. All of this is—at least 99 percent of the time—hypothetical. If something were actually chasing after us, we wouldn't have much time for stressing out about it—we'd be running!

We know the sensations that accompany that fight-or-flight reaction. For me, I feel my jaw clench, my shoulders tense up, and a general "buzzy" agitation all over my body. You may experience it as tight fists, restlessness, hypervigilance, twitching, and a compulsion to move, among other symptoms. Adrenaline may be coursing through your veins. This is what the sympathetic nervous system feels like when activated, and its purpose is to put you into action to deal with a threat.

Coming back into presence—which is your natural state as a spiritual being—begins to soothe your body and mind and turns on the parasympathetic nervous system (**p**arasympathetic brings about **p**eace is the reminder I use). This aspect of the nervous system initiates the "rest and digest" phase: it relaxes us. When we see the simplicity of this moment and connect to reality around us as it is, rather than what we project on it, the parasympathetic takes over, body/mind relaxes, and anxiety can be calmed.

Using Our Senses

Now, you may be wondering: "All right, how do I become more present? I can't just stop my thoughts and be here." You're right—trying to stop the thoughts isn't usually effective. It's more effective to shift our attention away from thoughts and to something else *concrete*.

The most helpful and efficient way I have found to do this is through our senses. Increasing sensory awareness helps to quiet the mind, or at least decreases the influence it has on us. This can be done by tuning in to specific sense elements.

Give it a shot right now. Touch something in your vicinity—maybe your own arm, for example. What does it feel like? Is the skin soft or rough? Is it dry, sweaty, smooth, or wrinkled? Are there soft hairs that you can detect under your fingers? Is your arm warm or cool to the touch? How does it feel to be touched—can you feel the warmth of the touching hand on the arm that is being touched? You might even feel some energy where you are touching, or perhaps a pulse.

Notice what you feel while doing this. Notice the mind. If you're really engaged with the sensory experience, the mind will not be very active. You can try this with any of the senses. Take in what you see around you—color, shading, texture, shapes, movement. What do you hear in this moment? Do you hear sounds nearby, faraway sounds, sounds muffled by a wall? Engage your sense of smell by holding a piece of

chocolate near your nostrils. Then let it sit on your tongue
and feel texture, temperature, and sweet or bitter flavors
beginning to resound through your mouth.

Don't Tell a Story—Use the Neutral Witness

If by chance you were feeling anxiety as you explored this,
it's likely that you were telling yourself a story as you did the
exercise. This isn't the same as using your inner witness—a
neutral observer mentioned in the last chapter—to engage
your senses.

When we're neutral and witnessing, we are simply reporting
facts, for lack of a more "spiritual" word. Ice is cold. The sun
is bright. Cars make a noise, perhaps a roaring noise. This is
different than narrating the experience. Here are some examples
of narrating these very same observations:

*"Oh, I'm so terribly cold, and I can't stand this ice on me
any longer. It's going to cause me to go numb or freeze my
fingers off!"*

*"The sun is just too bright and hot today. I hate it when I'm all
sweaty. Everything is drying up to a crisp—we haven't had rain
in weeks. It's a terrible drought, and we're all going to suffer!"*

*"This place is always so noisy. I hate all the cars that drive by
here constantly. They have allowed way too much expansion
in this city, and now we have too many people here. I
feel claustrophobic."*

You can see the difference between simple observation from the neutral witness—just reporting what is happening now—and the stories we may be telling ourselves about what we're experiencing.

Instead of stories, really get into experiencing the sensations. Don't make judgments. The sun may feel hot. That's neither good nor bad, it's just how you're experiencing it. When you can be honest with yourself about that, you can choose to either do something about it or not, but it won't have power over you. Eventually, won't even need to label things as "hot" or "cold." In presence, you will simply *be* with what is, as it is, and the mind will be silent.

You may discover that not only will the mind tend to calm when you simply allow yourself sensory experience in the present moment, but you might enjoy it. Our senses exist not just for our survival, but also for our pleasure. When we are experiencing more pleasure, our anxiety doesn't have room to enter.

Mindfulness

We've talked about how presence calms us because it brings us into the *now* through our senses. When we put that together with being in the mode of the neutral witness, we can rein in the tendency to project into the future or project our worries onto something outside of us. This practice is also known as mindfulness.

Let's say, for example, that you're feeling pain right now. The instinctual response is to try to stop the pain, which is a healthy response—we might need medical attention, to stop doing something that is hurting us, or to take a rest rather than push on.

But let's say that the pain remains after you've taken some action. This is when anxiety tends to rise, because we want the pain to go away! But as we explored in the last chapter, resisting tends to increase what we resist. In this case, the pain will tend to increase.

To be more specific, the pain itself may not increase, but our *experience* of the pain does. If we're focused on how bad and awful it is, how we don't like it, that it must stop, and "Oh my gosh, what will happen if it gets worse," then we're going to have a pretty dreadful experience of that pain.

Numerous studies (https://nccih.nih.gov/research/blog/mindfulness-meditation-pain) demonstrate how mindfulness can effectively reduce the experience of pain, both physical and emotional, not only by learning to observe physical sensations and sensory experiences, but also by learning to observe our own emotions and even thoughts. Learning to do this with that neutral witness within will help us to soften the experience of anxiety and return us to calm, grounded presence.

We will go through how to be in the mode of that neutral witness to feel your anxiety in a new way in Chapter 12, "Feeling Your Anxiety." For now, work with the practice of presence as often as you can remember to engage with it in your day-to-day life. It will become more potent and easier as you add the next key to calming your anxiety: embodiment.

Chapter 11

Embodiment

*"At every stage of spiritual growth, the greatest ally
you have is your body."*

—Deepak Chopra

To calm your anxiety, it is essential that you become embodied.
I can't emphasize this enough. I know many people who deal
with their anxiety by leaving their bodies. Temporarily, this can
seem to help. But as a habit of dealing with upset, it actually
perpetuates the cycle of anxiety.

Before I explain why embodiment is so important, how it
perpetuates the anxiety if you're disembodied, and ways that you
can feel embodied, let's make sure we're on the same page.

What Is Embodiment?

It may seem kind of weird to think about whether we're in our
bodies or not. How can I possibly not be in my body—I'm here,
aren't I? I have a body and I move around in it, I feed it, I sleep
in it. I run half-marathons, swim, play basketball, or do yoga.
Doesn't that mean that I'm embodied?

No, it doesn't. We can do all those things and not be fully
embodied. In fact, sometimes we can be almost completely
disembodied while doing some of these activities. It's like
running your yoga poses by remote control. And that has some
consequences. We've explored some of those consequences in
Chapter 5—the spiritual mistake of habitually leaving the body.

Embodiment, in the context of this book, means you are fully present and aware *inside* your body. It refers to experiencing *what is* through your bodily awareness. It is key to presence, because without embodiment, you can't accurately experience what *is* in this three-dimensional world. You can only *think about* it, imagine it, or observe it.

Feeling the Experience

To transform anxiety, you need to be able to actually *feel* it. It is not about avoiding it or pushing it away. And we feel through the body. It's an instrument designed specifically for sensing what is happening to and around you.

Through these first three chapters of Part III, we are building the foundations necessary to be able to feel the anxiety without becoming overwhelmed by it. Two things are going on there— feeling and being overwhelmed. One happens in the body: the actual feelings. The other happens in the mind: the sense of being overwhelmed. Contrary to what we believe, being overwhelmed isn't caused by the actual physical experience of anxiety. It results from how we *think about* what we're experiencing. If we stay in our heads and leave our bodies, the only thing we're really left with is thinking—and if our thinking is focused on how overwhelming it is, worry, anticipation of bad things happening, and so on, it will be very difficult to calm down.

From Inside the Body

Embodiment involves shifting our experience from outside to inside. Often, when we're trying to avoid our anxiety, a subtle shift of awareness happens. We might begin to look at ourselves from the outside. This disconnects us from the experience we're having. This is called *dissociation*.

This isn't always a bad thing—sometimes it can be helpful to get a little distance from constantly monitoring what is happening within ourselves. But as a habit, and especially as a continual strategy for dealing with fear, it has drawbacks. The main liability is that we don't get as accurate a read on what's going on when we're *looking at ourselves from outside* rather than *experiencing from inside*.

An Experiment

I've noticed this tendency in myself to observe and feel my body from an outside perspective, rather than from inside. Here's an experiment which I've done, and you can, too.

I usually brush my teeth over a sink in front of a mirror, probably a lot like you do. I'd like for you to look in the mirror as you brush your teeth. Watch where the toothbrush is moving around your mouth, and while looking at the reflection of where it is, notice what you feel. Locate the feeling *by looking in the mirror* at what is happening and where you're brushing. How connected do you feel to your teeth, your gums, the movement of the toothbrush, the feeling of the toothpaste in your mouth?

Now, brush your teeth again. But this time, close your eyes. Feel inside your mouth. Feel the sensation of the toothbrush bristles rubbing on the teeth and gums. What is it like now? Is the experience more or less intense or palpable than before?

Do you notice the toothpaste foaming up—what is that like?
How about the flavor of the toothpaste? Can you feel that
on your tongue? Maybe you can even notice where on your
tongue you pick up on that flavor. How about the feeling of
holding the brush in your hand, and the action of the muscles
that move the toothbrush? Can you feel these sensations from
the perspective of being inside your mouth, fingers, hand, and
arm rather than looking at it from outside?

Chances are good that your experience was similar to mine. I
became much more aware of sensations and the experience of
brushing my teeth when my eyes were closed. What surprised
me, though, wasn't just the increase in awareness, but how
different it felt to sense it from inside my body, rather than
watching it from outside my body. I couldn't describe that
difference, but it was startling. I wondered how often I *watch*
what I am doing rather than being inside of myself, engaged in
the experience of doing it.

You can learn to be inside your body—to be embodied—through
some simple practices. If done consistently, you'll feel more
at home inside your own body and will be able to ease and
transform anxiety more readily.

Centering

I am pretty sure you've heard of centering before. If you have,
great—this is a reminder for you, and perhaps you'll learn some
new perspectives on how to experience your center. But please
don't skip this even if you think you know it. Most of us on
the spiritual path have a lot of tools that we know, but which

we forget to use (or just don't take the time to). Believe me, centering is the best tool for calming anxiety—I've consistently seen it help clients and students, again and again, return to their feeling of peace within.

Centering is a way of finding your sense of self. It's like a home base in the body for what you describe as "you." When we center, we are bringing our energy and attention back into the core of the body. Centering helps organize our experience of ourselves and the world. Without a center from which to look out at life, we can end up feeling scattered—like we've fallen apart—which naturally increases anxiety, fear, and agitation.

Part of centering relates to what is called our *core*. The core is something that is talked about a lot in Pilates, yoga, and dance. It is the energetic central axis around which you organize yourself.

Connecting with your core is a subtle experience (centering, in general, is a subtle practice), and it may require some patience to get the hang of it. Steven Kessler, author of *The 5 Personality Patterns*, acknowledges that while it can take time to attune yourself to your core, it's essential for centering. "It is what gives you a felt sense of self. It is required for referencing yourself and perceiving what you actually feel and want."

When we're worried and anxious, our sense of self is often spread out, or even shattered, into little pieces of worry about this relationship over here, stress at work over there, the political situation way out there, and the health of our parents or kids back over there. Our energy goes out to all these thoughts and external circumstances, and this can leave us feeling empty and distraught within.

A Case Study

Leslie always came to sessions dressed to the nines. With her high-end business suits and impeccably polished nails, she was very much the image of a high-powered account executive for a financial company. In addition to the stress of her demanding career, one of the issues that Leslie struggled with was her anxiety after a painful breakup. Her last lover, whom she had a deep, intimate connection with, had ended the relationship rather abruptly, and she felt confused, deceived, and very alone.

She frequently found herself tense and anxious. Once, as we were working with embodiment practices, she described her experience as "scattered," as if her sense of self were going out in many directions.

It was a familiar feeling—she was used to extending herself out to the people she cared about and the many projects she managed at work. But it also felt empty, like a "void" inside her, which increased her anxiety and feeling of loneliness. She recognized that this habit of connecting with others by scattering bits of herself out to them hurt: she ended up feeling misunderstood, even rejected, and experiencing loss of her sense of self.

As I walked her through drawing her energy back into her core and her center, at first she was a bit uncomfortable. This was an unfamiliar experience. She wasn't feeling connection in the way she was used to. But as we circled around to return all her scattered energy into her center a second time, a calmness came over her. The stress and the anxiety, much to her surprise, were released. She felt capable of dealing with the challenges of the day, and she recognized that she didn't have to lose her center or her sense of self in order to make connections with those she cared about.

Simple Centering Practice

Centering can be simple and easy if you allow it to be. Don't worry if you believe you haven't "got it" in the past. Trust that by your intent, you'll find your center within.

The easiest way I have found to center is placing my hands on my belly. Imagine a warm ball of energy in the middle of your belly, just below the navel and back toward the spine. Feel, see, and sense it there, glowing. This is the gravitational center of your body, i.e., the part of the body which balances above and below. If you're centered here, you'll feel more stable and be able to balance better—whether on one foot, like in the yogic Tree pose, or on two. Martial artists are usually taught to center themselves in a similar way.

Now, imagine that energy extends from your belly down to your tailbone and up through the front of your spine to the crown of your head. By extending the energy of your center up and down in something like a tube or column of light, you're creating the sense of your core. Feel this central energetic axis of yourself, or try to imagine it.

The final step here in this process, which is most helpful for anxiety yet is not often included in most centering practices, is calling your energy back. Imagine all the ways in which your thoughts and emotions might be scattered right now. Picture energetic filaments of light extending from your center and core out to all those people, situations, beliefs, and ideas about your past or your future.

Now, call all that energy back to you. State that you are now calling back all the energy, thought, and emotion that you put out there and reclaiming that energy. It's you, and it doesn't belong out there. Don't worry—you'll still be able to attend to all that stuff. In fact, you'll be able to *respond* better (rather than *react*) without anxiety by having all your personal energy back inside your center, where it belongs.

Visualize all of it coming back, and feel it filling your core up within. Experience the wholeness of *you* returning. Breathe it in and allow it to settle within you. Notice what it feels like to have all of yourself back. Check in with the anxiety: has it lessened? Likely it will be so. But even if it hasn't, this practice will equip you to better deal with anything that causes you fear or worry, because you'll have all of your capacity centered within you, where it's more available to create helpful, intelligent responses to life stressors.

Grounding

Now that you're centered and your energy is reclaimed back into your body, we can take the next step of embodiment—*grounding*. Grounding is our intentional connection to the earth, this planet that we live on. It further stabilizes us and our personal energy and links us to a greater source of energy than our own personal life force.

Trees are an excellent example of being grounded. Out of necessity, trees send roots down deep into the earth. These roots serve multiple purposes: to be able to draw nutrients up from the soil, to connect to the network of the forest, to stabilize, and to draw on the great supporter of life, the very heart of our planet earth.

Rooting down is what allows trees to stabilize but also to grow upwards. If they weren't solidly rooted into the soil, trees would simply topple over. We humans aren't that different. But we believe we are, especially when we're on the spiritual path. We tend to assume that if we just connect to the heavenly realms, the upper chakras, and the center of the cosmos, we'll progress and everything in life will be taken care of as a matter of course.

However, our Divine expansion needs grounding in our planetary mother as long as each of us is here in a body, just as every other living being needs to be connected with the earth. In order to expand out into the realm of spirit and sustain our earthly bodies, we need to ground. Agitation, unsteadiness, hypersensitivity, and yes, anxiety, are the emotional equivalents of toppling over like an unrooted tree.

How to Ground

I learned my favorite grounding technique (and some of the other practices in this chapter) from my energy work teacher, Lynda Caesara, based in Berkeley, CA (she credits them to her years of training as a psychic). This way of grounding is simple, and, with practice, you'll be able to do it fairly quickly.

Stand with your feet hip width apart, or sit in a chair with your feet flat on the floor. Feel your energetic center in your belly. From that point, imagine extending energetic roots down through each of your legs as well as one down through your tailbone. Allow those roots to grow out of the base of the spine and the soles of your feet, down into the earth.

Send those energetic roots deep into the soil, down past the rock, down past the molten lava, down to the absolute core of the earth. Then, imagine them wrapping around something

very solid there, perhaps a boulder or the iron crystal that is
said to be at the center of the planet.

Once anchored there, allow the energy of the earth mother
to rise effortlessly and naturally up into your body. Feel the
stabilizing, nurturing, supportive earth energy filling every
cell and surrounding you in a protective energy. This is an
unlimited source of healing, soothing, and stabilizing energy
that you can tap into anytime to calm and steady yourself,
whatever may be happening in your life.

The Third Component: Boundaries

The third essential component of becoming embodied is
boundaries. Of course, there are many kinds of boundaries we
could discuss here—setting boundaries with a coworker or your
kid or being clear about what time you'll be available to see a
client and how long the appointment will be. But in this case,
for this book, I'm focusing on something more subtle, and yet
necessary to feel fully embodied: energetic boundaries.

Having an energetic boundary means that you're aware of where
your energy starts and ends...and where you might interface with
other people's energy. A healthy energetic boundary helps us
feel safe in our physical body and allows our nervous system to
relax more.

Your Edge

Any kind of boundary, whether is it around the property where you live or around your personal body, needs to have an edge—a place where you know your personal energy extends to. Anything inside that boundary is "you"; anything outside is "not you."

This is a critical element for spiritual folks, because many of us are Highly Sensitive Persons (HSPs) or empaths. We naturally pick up on the thoughts, emotions, and energies of other people. If we aren't conscious about this, we may go through our days and nights absorbing other people's stuff like sponges (See Chapter 7).

When we take on other people's emotions, thoughts, perceptions, and energies, it can feel like when we've eaten unhealthy or even spoiled food. We might feel angry when nothing has precipitated it. We feel the suffering of children and their families in war-torn countries. It is all too easy to take on the pain and anguish of anyone else we come in contact with, either in our physical space or that we read, see, or hear about through media. Taking on what isn't yours is almost guaranteed to increase your anxiety.

Noticing Your Energy Field

Many people aren't aware of their energy field, but being that you're on the spiritual path, you may be familiar with it. Also known as your aura, it extends out around you in all directions, including above and below, front and back, and side to side. You might visualize it, feel it as a vibration, or perhaps you simply intuit or sense it being there.

Make note of how far it extends from your body. If it's very close to your skin, you're not claiming enough space for yourself in this world. You deserve to have an energetic space around you, and it's essential for your well-being.

If you only have a centimeter of your energy field around you, it creates certain challenges. One is that other people's energy will easily come in very close to you, which can be disturbing and set off your anxiety. Even with people you care about, having their energy that close to you all the time is hard on your system. It's like trying to run all of the electrical outlets, with the appliances plugged into them, for your own house *and* having to deal with the energy demands of all the appliances and lighting for your neighbor's house, too. One electrical system for one home isn't set up for that.

The other challenge that having only a very narrow band of energy around you creates is that people will have to come in close to you in order to reach and connect to you. Because your energetic vibration, so to speak, isn't extending out very far, people can't quite pick up on you. In fact, you might even notice that people bump into you a lot accidentally. It's not necessarily a coincidence—they simply may not be able to pick up on your vibration!

One time, I was taking a class on energy awareness and I experienced this very dilemma. I was sitting on the floor with my legs tucked under me and my feet off to the side. A much larger woman with bigger energy walked by, and her toenail scraped my foot. I winced but tried not to make any noise so I wouldn't disrupt the class. My foot was bleeding, but she didn't even notice she had bumped into me! When I remarked about this to my teacher, she looked at me compassionately and said, "Well, it's because she can't feel that you're there."

In order to be *here*, to be embodied, to be fully engaged with the world and for the world to fully engage with you, you need a healthy energy field. So if it's only an inch or two from your body, we're going to work on extending it out about two to three feet in each direction.

A Field That's Too Big

Now, you could be running into the other end of an energetic boundary problem: it might be too big. You may find that your energy fills up entire rooms. You may have the problem that my classmate had—walking into the room and not attending to *other* people's energetic space.

Sometimes, people on the spiritual path are used to expanding their energy and sending it out in subtle ways to reach others. We might use tools to build it through breathwork, meditation, visualization, or tantric practices. But if we're building our energy so much that it begins to take over everyone else's energetic space, we begin to lose our connection to embodiment by expanding into infinity. The challenge this poses is that others may feel their territory is being encroached upon. They may feel uncomfortable or overwhelmed by our big energy.

If your anxiety is triggered by others either withdrawing from you or pushing back on your energetic space, it's possible that you have too large of an energetic boundary. Or, alternatively, your field may be so big that you have a hard time distinguishing your own energy from others and end up merging it into everyone around you—and once again, likely picking up whatever disturbances are in their psyche.

So if you sense that your vibrational field is often six, seven, or eight feet around you or more, part of your embodiment practice is to bring it back in to about two to three feet around you and to develop a palpable edge or boundary delineating your sense of self.

Creating Your Energetic Boundary

The solution is to develop a clear energetic boundary for yourself. This can be very unfamiliar for those who are accustomed and even a bit attached to feeling everyone else's feelings for themselves. Yet the benefits—reducing your anxiety and allowing you to feel more ease—are worth the effort.

Are you willing to experiment and practice? Remember, practice takes time, repetition, and consistency to become masterful. And if we bring in nonattachment as well, it will be easier to let go of the habit of absorbing other's experiences and to let go of needing to get this "boundary thing" perfect right off the bat.

Imagine that you're surrounded by a circle of light. You can make that band of light any color that feels strong and vibrant for you—white, gold, and blue are good choices if you're not sure. Notice how close the circle of light is to you. Also be aware of how clear or diffuse it is. Is there a well-defined edge, or does it blur out indefinitely? Attempt to refine it into a clear, steady, boundary about two to three feet around you.

Now, picture that energetic edge around you in all directions, so that it becomes a sphere of light. See the entire sphere around you (or feel it, or just know that it's there) about three feet in every direction. Imagine drawing energy up from the earth (refer to the grounding exercise) to fill the entire space inside with that light, including your own physical body. Now you can do the grounding and centering exercises and let the earth energy rise up through your roots and then emanate out from your core to fill your body and energy field.

Me/Not Me

Notice how it feels to have this energy all around you. Observe the increased clarity about your center and your edge. What is inside that boundary is you, and nothing else is allowed. What is outside that boundary is *not* you. Lynda Caesara calls this awareness and practice "Me/Not Me."

You may have done a similar practice for creating a shield of protection around you, for indeed, energetic boundaries serve as protection. But they also clarify your sense of who you are in this body, in this space that you're currently inhabiting on planet earth.

Energetic boundaries additionally serve as your energetic skin. You can interact with the world from the edge of your boundary. This protects you from unwanted energies, while at the same time, it more keenly develops your ability to sense energy in your vicinity.

I like using the metaphor of a house with a garden. You are the house. That's your domain, your private space of *you*. You wouldn't want any stranger just walking in your door, going to your refrigerator, and eating your leftovers! So you have a door that locks. But even having strangers come all the way up to your door probably feels a bit uncomfortable. That's like having a very small, thin energy field around you.

To feel more embodied and secure in your energetic space, extend your edge out even more. Picture a yard in front of your house. It has a small fence around it with a gate. People can see in but can't enter except through the gate. And you are the keeper of the gate.

When a friend, neighbor, or stranger arrives, rather than letting them walk all the way up to your door and maybe even peep in the window, they wait at the gate. You are in your house or front yard, and you know what's inside the gate is *you*; anyone approaching the gate is clearly *not-you*. You consciously decide how much to interact with them and how close to allow them to come.

Because you are attending to your edge and feeling the presence of whose energy is around you (or learning to do that!), you recognize there's someone at your gate, so you come out to meet them there. You can have a conversation with them at the gate, or maybe even invite them into your front yard to sit for a chat. But you are in charge. You would only let those who you deeply trust and are very intimate with to enter in your front door.

So the edge of your aura becomes your energetic skin. You can feel what's going on outside from that boundary about two to three feet around you. You no longer have to let everything come in and overwhelm you, and you can still pick up on what's happening out there—maybe even more clearly and quickly than you did before.

Becoming Fully *Here*

By centering yourself, grounding to the earth, and clarifying your
energetic boundary, you become fully *here*. You know who you
are and can palpably feel who you are. You can feel connected to
the planet and therefore more secure and safe. Your energy feels
more consistently full and strong and is clearly distinguished
from everything else happening out in the universe. This
combination calms down the nervous system quite effectively
if you practice, practice, practice. From that place of calm and
embodiment, you can then expand into Divine realms and know
where you're returning to.

Chapter 12

Self-Compassion

*"That is what compassion does. It challenges
our assumptions, our sense of self-limitation,
worthlessness, of not having a place in the world. As
we develop compassion, our hearts open."*

—Sharon Salzberg

The most essential practice for calming anxiety is self-compassion. Without it, we run the risk of continually beating ourselves up with worry and self-abnegation. It's easy to become critical of ourselves and anxious about *having* anxiety. Self-compassion helps to shift us out of those self-harming tendencies. It is an embodiment of *maitri*, being a good friend to ourselves, or as the Buddhists define it, loving-kindness.

The Sanskrit word for compassion is *karuna*. In the *Yoga Sutras*, we are directed to practice compassion toward those who are suffering. This can not only be helpful to those around us who are in pain, but Patanjali, the author of the yoga sutras, asserts that this practice will help us maintain inner serenity, even when we see others who are unhappy.

The Yoga Sutras treat *maitri* and *karuna* as separate practices: with people who are happy, we practice friendliness (*maitri*) toward them, and with those who are sad, we extend *karuna*. These are keys to maintaining inner serenity, no matter what situation in life arises in front of us.

But truthfully, *maitri* and *karuna* go hand in hand—especially when dealing with a challenging emotion within ourselves, like fear. In order to practice compassion with anyone, including

ourselves, we need to embody the quality of friendliness
toward them.

Remember this when exploring self-compassion practice. Think
about how you would want someone else to be with you when
you're feeling fear—or how you yourself would be with a loved
one. You certainly wouldn't want someone to tell you to just
get rid of it. You wouldn't want them to say, "I can't stand that
you're feeling this anxiety, it's too much for me, get out of here!"
Yet we often do this to ourselves. We berate ourselves for having
the anxiety and want to make it go away. That's not being very
friendly, is it?

We often forget that the very spiritual concepts that are intended
to be practiced with others are also meant to be applied to how
we treat ourselves. It's important to be a good friend to yourself,
and you deserve compassion, too. You are worthy of that care
and kindness. The challenge is learning how to do that for
yourself—and that is something you *can* learn.

Why Do Self-Compassion?

You may think, well, compassion is important for giving to
others, but why would I do it for myself? Wouldn't I become
lazy? Isn't that just indulgence in my emotions? Shouldn't I just
try to get rid of that worry and fear?

Kristin Neff, PhD, author of *Self-Compassion: The Proven
Power of Being Kind to Yourself* and internationally recognized
expert on self-compassion, has a lot to say about the importance
of practicing it. She asserts, "Many people believe that they
need to be self-critical to motivate themselves, but in fact they
just end up feeling anxious, incompetent, and depressed." In

fact, Dr. Neff has been studying self-compassion for over fifteen years, and her research shows that "far from encouraging self-indulgence, self-compassion helps us to see ourselves clearly and make needed changes because we care about ourselves and want to reach our full potential."

Especially for people with anxiety, self-compassion is vital to reducing those overwhelming, stressed-out feelings. It helps return us to a feeling of well-being, acceptance of ourselves, and feeling more capable and resilient.

What Is Compassion?

But first, let's understand what I am referring to as compassion: *karuna*. We might believe that compassion is sympathy or pity. It isn't.

Reverend Michael Bernard Beckwith, bestselling author of *The Life Visioning Process* and leader in the New Thought movement, lends us some clarity about the differences between sympathy, empathy, and compassion. I'll share some of his concepts about this here, with a bit of elaboration and additions of my own.

Sympathy, he says, essentially is an expression of the thought, "I feel *sorry* for you." It's not empowering for either the giver or receiver of the sympathy. It is basically asserting that someone is in an awful situation and isn't that a pity. It's a sorry state of affairs. There's nothing really transformative about sympathy that will effectively shift you out of anxiety. If you feel sympathy for yourself, you're likely to end up in a pity party. This is probably not what you hoped for when you picked up this book.

Empathy sounds like a better choice. But empathy, according to Beckwith, translates as "I'll feel *for* you." When we have empathy, we're literally taking on someone else's emotions and feeling them for ourselves. This can throw our systems off balance, and actually, being overly empathic can contribute to your anxiety. If you're taking on the pain and suffering of the world (as we touched on in the "Embodiment" chapter), you risk triggering feelings of despair and being overwhelmed, and anxiety can go through the roof. Therefore, although empathy is a helpful skill, it's not the best choice if you're trying to overcome the cycle of anxiety. And if we're looking at being empathic toward ourselves, then we're essentially just feeling our anxiety over and over, without any resolution.

But compassion, Beckwith says, is different. It has the capacity to open the giver and receiver of compassion in new ways. There are several aspects to compassion. The first is to be *openhearted*. To truly express and embody compassion, our hearts must be open to the other, and in this case, to ourselves. This is not the same as taking on their emotions as our own; it is rather the willingness to bear witness to their pain (and your own). Compassion asks us to *listen* to the one suffering, and following this chapter, we will spend two chapters on how to feel and listen to your anxiety. Listening requires being fully *present*, which we have explored in Chapter 9.

Then, being compassionate asks us to cultivate *understanding* of the one who suffers. We endeavor to truly comprehend the suffering someone is experiencing to the best of our ability, and in listening to our own anxiety, we learn to do that for ourselves. As we develop understanding, we show that we *care* about the one who is in pain or despair. This chapter will show you how to extend that caring to your very own self. Lastly, compassion asks us to take one more step and ask *how can I serve?* We consider in what way we might make a difference for the one who is suffering, whether that is as simple as prayer, making a donation, or volunteering at a soup kitchen. For ourselves, we might consider: what kind of action could I take to alleviate, shift, or transform this anxiety? Chapters 15 and 16 focus on this skill.

So, to review, these are the components of a truly self-compassionate approach to our anxiety:

· Openheartedness
· Presence
· Listening
· Understanding
· Caring
· Serving (a transforming action)

How might you open your heart to your own fears or worries right now? Take some time to be present and listen to your suffering. What do you understand about this anxiety? Making time to do this demonstrates to yourself that you care, which is self-soothing and comforting in itself. And then consider what would be helpful for you in healing and releasing this anxiety. Don't worry, these steps are coming in the following chapters if you don't get all that right now.

Compassion Is a Self-Soothing Practice

Compassion is one of the ways that you can soothe yourself when you're upset or stressed out. Self-soothing is a skill that goes all the way back to the crib. As babies, we needed to learn to soothe ourselves enough that we could fall asleep. Some self-soothing techniques that are probably familiar from your own childhood are thumb or pacifier sucking, having a favorite "lovey" object such as a stuffed animal or blanket, listening to soothing music, and having a special nighttime ritual, like having a story read to you before bed.

We still need to be able to self-soothe when we're adults in order to go to sleep—and to calm anxiety. Some of the things we do as adults to self-soothe are taking a bath or shower, drinking some herbal tea, lighting a fire in the fireplace, reading a book, and listening to music. There are some forms of self-soothing that are detrimental for us, like overeating or drinking alcohol. So it's very important to develop healthy ways to soothe yourself and bring calm back into your life.

When we have challenges with anxiety, it may be due to not having been soothed sufficiently when we were young. Maybe your parents weren't there for you in the way you needed them to be. You might have been left alone a lot, or even harshly treated. You might not have received enough touch. This can cause a belief to develop within us that no one is there to comfort us. On top of that, we didn't learn ways to comfort ourselves, or attempted to do so with unhealthy means.

Fortunately, no matter what your early life was like, we can all learn to soothe and comfort ourselves and encourage that relaxation response in our nervous system. It takes some effort (remember: practice, not perfection!), but is well worth it to calm your anxiety.

Here's a few ways in addition to self-compassion that you can soothe yourself:

· Spend a few minutes doing yoga poses
· Practice deep breathing
· Do a relaxing guided visualization or meditation

· Go for a walk
· Stand in the rain (as long as you're not too cold!), or listen to it on the roof
· Pet your dog or cat
· Get a massage
· Take a bath (bubbles optional!) or hot shower
· Massage your feet (or have a partner do it for you!)
· Brush your hair (this can be surprisingly calming)
· Massage acupressure points on the face
· Have some chamomile tea
· Listen to calming music
· Talk to a loved one
· Sit outdoors in nature (or your garden or local park)
· Wrap yourself in a cozy blanket
· Hugs, cuddles, and snuggles!

What do you do to self-soothe? Write it down. Use the list to help calm yourself when you feel anxiety. I'd love to hear your self-soothing list—send it to me at Connie@AwakeningSelf.com. Now, let's add self-compassion to the list.

A Self-Compassion Exercise

Ready to try on some self-compassion? Good. Make yourself comfortable. If you're chilly, wrap yourself up in a warm blanket. That will start the process of soothing and make self-compassion more accessible.

Put your hands on your heart, in the center of your chest. Or you can put one hand on your heart and the other on your belly. Let the touch of your own hands give you comfort.

Breathe deeply and gently—no need to make a lot of effort, but draw in enough to open up the lungs and slow the breath down. The slower you breathe, the more likely you will feel relaxed and at ease. In particular, let the exhalations lengthen just a bit.

Now, notice the anxiety within you. Practicing *maitri*, be there for yourself as you would for a good friend who might hold your hand or put a hand on your shoulder. They would simply listen and maybe offer some support like, "I can see how hard this is for you. I'm here if you need me." Be there for yourself. It is possible.

Feel free to use your own words. What other comforting words might you say to yourself? "I am right here with you in this worry and fear. I know it's hard. I am right here for you." Talk to yourself like you would to a young child who was feeling this way. Feel that compassion—that *karuna*—for yourself.

Then, take this beyond only yourself. Contemplate all the billions of people on the planet who certainly feel or have felt what you're feeling. Say to yourself, "I am feeling anxiety right now. I understand that I am suffering and that others suffer with this anxiety like me." You're not alone. You're not the only one in the universe who deals with this. You are part of a shared human experience. And like those other people who struggle with their fears, worries, stress, and feelings of being overwhelmed, you will find your way through this. You have that capacity inside, and you will find your way as you journey through this book.

Extending Self-Compassion into Self-Forgiveness

Self-compassion can flow naturally into the state of self-forgiveness, forgiving yourself first of all for having the anxiety in the first place. As we just touched on, anxiety is a normal human emotion that comes up from time to time. The fact that your anxiety might feel out of control may be in part because you haven't yet accepted your humanness. You're allowed to have difficulties and struggles and to make mis-takes . It's part of life, and it's actually *expected*. If you don't, you really should be in the angelic realms, and not here on earth (wink).

On the spiritual path, we may believe that we should be beyond anxiety and fear. We think we "should" be serene and calm now, as we touched on in the Spiritual Mis-takes section. But just because you're spiritual doesn't mean you won't still have issues like this arise. The difference is that on the spiritual path, you will utilize all of your experiences—including anxiety—for your awakening.

Consider the fact that you cannot learn and grow if you don't make mis-takes —it's not possible! A perfect life will offer no opportunities for moving past your edge of familiarity and comfort. There would never be anything truly new. Maybe you could reframe (a technique of gaining a new perspective on an issue) this experience: it is opening you up to new vistas in your life.

Remembering this might help you to forgive yourself for a mistake you made that triggered anxiety in you. This is all par for the course. You're actually right on track. One of my coaches, Angela Lauria, reminds us often that life doesn't happen *to* you— it happens *for* you. It happens for your continued evolution and expansion into greater possibilities. The fact that this anxiety has arisen now is an opportunity for you to evolve and awaken more deeply; it's not a sign that you've done something wrong. In fact, by reading this book and taking action in your life to heal and transform it, you're definitely doing something right.

Consider forgiving yourself for any aspect of this anxiety—for having it, for judging yourself, for fearing the judgment of others, for believing you're less-than, or for not trusting the Universe enough. Whatever it is, by allowing self-forgiveness to happen, you will go a long way toward releasing this anxiety. That's a very self-compassionate step to take.

Chapter 13

Feeling Your Anxiety

"You don't have to control your thoughts. You just have to stop letting them control you."

—Dan Millman

Now, it's time to feel your anxiety. What, you say? I already feel my anxiety too much! I want to *stop* feeling anxiety! What are you doing???

I understand that this sounds completely ass-backward. It's counterintuitive, but the truth is that until you can truly feel your anxiety, you probably won't be able to release your anxiety. Let me explain.

Feeling vs. Thinking Your Anxiety

Chances are, you aren't really *feeling* your anxiety—you're *thinking* your anxiety. The difference between these two ways of experiencing your emotions (not just anxiety, but all of them) makes all the difference in the world in being able to overcome anxiety.

Feeling an emotion is going beyond thought. Most of the time, when we say we're feeling something, we're actually telling stories about what we're feeling. For example, anxiety may arise, and then we go on a rampage. A story we might tell could sound something like this:

I'm feeling so stressed about teaching this yoga class! I'm a substitute teacher, and they probably won't like me. Why would they? I expect my teachers to be there when I go to classes, and I'm always disappointed when a substitute shows up. They'll probably all frown when they see me. I'm not good enough, anyway, and they'll be able to tell. And what if I don't know what to say, or forget what I had planned to do next? I'll look like a fool, and they'll wonder what I'm doing teaching. This is going to be awful.

Is any of that actually feeling? No, that's engaging in the thoughts and letting them run. I call this *Getting on the Train*. You may start out with feeling nervous, and then you get on this anxious train of thought, and it gets worse.

You start in New York, let's say. But then, with each successive thought that adds to the story—usually about what we *think* will happen, not what is actually happening—before you know it, you're in Chicago or Denver or all the way to the West Coast. Far from home, and far away from finding courage and calm within. When we finally get off the train (if we ever do!), our anxiety has increased substantially, and it may have nothing to do with reality.

Awareness of the Stories

How do we break this cycle and find the inner peace and ease we long for? We need to become aware of the tendency to tell stories about who we are and what we're experiencing that increase anxiety.

Don Miguel Ruiz, Toltec shaman and bestselling author, calls this tendency to tell stories about our experience (what I call *thinking* our anxiety) the "voice of knowledge." In his book *The Voice of Knowledge*, he states:

"What you call thinking is the voice of knowledge making up stories, telling you what you know, and trying to make sense out of everything you don't know. The problem is that the voice makes you do many things that go against yourself... When the voice in your head finally stops talking, you experience *inner peace*."

In yogic philosophy, Ruiz is referring to what is called *nir-o-dha-h*. This is when all thoughts, all stories stop, and we experience union, Oneness. In that inner silence, only peace remains.

Understanding this tendency to tell stories and how it exacerbates your anxiety—and being able to get off the train of thought—is key to changing the pattern of fear, worry, and stress that creates your anxious experiences.

Emotions Are in the Body, Not the Mind

Truly and accurately feeling your anxiety—or any emotion—has a lot to do with body sensations, and very little to do with thoughts. You may employ the mind to identify what is going on: OK, I notice that I'm feeling anxious. I wonder what that is about? The mind should play a supportive role of keeping you on track with awareness of the process as you step off the train of thought and back into your felt experience of the emotion.

Emotions are actually sensations in the body. When you're feeling angry, for example, how do you know that? You may be frustrated that your kid contradicted you and said something disrespectful, but you know you're angry for sure when your voice becomes louder, you clench your teeth, your face gets hot, your neck is suddenly tense, or you begin to make fists. Otherwise, you're just thinking about it. Without body sensation, it's not emotion, it's just analysis.

Beyond Thought and Judgment

It's also important not to become judgmental when we're feeling an emotion. Judgment makes us feel like crap. That's not going to help release our anxiety one bit, and it's likely to make us more upset.

If you're feeling nervous about a job interview, for example, judging yourself for feeling nervous about it will send you down into the dumps. Self-talk like, "I shouldn't be feeling nervous" or "Oh, I'm so nervous, and that's a bad thing!" simply creates more anxiety, right?

If you're increasing your awareness of your anxiety, it's essential that you unplug the tendency to judge yourself about it *and* the tendency to judge the fact that you're judging! That is a surefire way to perpetuate what you're trying to release.

It *is* possible to notice the anxiety from the perspective of the neutral witness, as we explored in Chapter 8. Observe the anxiety from a place of simple awareness: *I am aware that I'm feeling afraid right now.* It is not good or bad, right nor wrong, it simply is, and all your judgment and condemnation about having that anxiety is only going to hinder your healing process.

Employ self-compassion as you increase your awareness. Everyone has anxiety from time to time. It's normal. Embrace yourself with that compassion as you notice yourself feeling anxious and as you notice thoughts that may arise from your worries and fears.

Welcome It In

It's time to stop pushing anxiety away and judging yourself for having anxiety; accept that it's here. Welcome it in. It has shown up, and you can either deny it and put off your transformation, or you can embrace it, accept the fact that it is present, and see what is here within you.

> *This being human is a guest house.*
> *Every morning a new arrival.*
>
> *A joy, a depression, a meanness,*
> *some momentary awareness comes*
> *as an unexpected visitor.*
>
> *Welcome and entertain them all!*
> *Even if they are a crowd of sorrows,*
> *who violently sweep your house*
> *empty of its furniture,*
> *still, treat each guest honorably.*
> *He may be clearing you out*
> *for some new delight.*
>
> *—Jellaludin Rumi,*
> *excerpt from translation by Coleman Barks*

Every emotion that shows up is a guest in our awareness. It's not who we are, but it's an experience we are having. Treat it like a guest in your home, with kindness and acceptance, and when we work with "Listening to Your Anxiety" in the next chapter, you'll be able to learn and grow from the experience rather than shrinking from it.

Acceptance—Letting Go of Hope

In her book *When Things Fall Apart*, author and Tibetan Buddhist nun Pema Chodron asserts that we need to give up hope. When I first read that, I thought, great. No hope. I'm going to be this way forever. That's depressing. I was angry, and I felt like throwing the book away. But I kept reading. And when I read the next line, I got it: "Without giving up hope—that there's somewhere better to be, that there's someone better to be—we will never relax with where we are or who we are."

It stopped me in my tracks. All this time, when I felt anxious or fearful, I just wanted everything to be different. I wanted *me* to be different. I didn't like me in that moment and was rejecting myself and everything around me. No wonder I felt anxious and horrible. Rejection was the last thing I needed, and it only served to worsen my anxiety.

The hope of it getting better, of things being other than how they were, was violence I was doing to myself. How can things be other than how they are in the moment? The only way is to embrace and accept how things are and then see what can arise next. Hope was a resistance and was making me wish for some magic wand rather than looking at the roots of my suffering.

It hit me that a lot of my anxiety was this very rejection of myself, over and over again. Not wanting life to be the way it was, not wanting myself to be the way I was. If I was to get over my anxiety, I needed to learn to accept. Only then, ironically, could things change. Only then could my internal experience of what was happening shift and the anxiety dissipate.

This is holding compassionate awareness of yourself and this moment, just as it is. When we do that, then we can actually feel our feelings, which gives them the right conditions to shift and change.

Everything Is Temporary

Now, when you're looking at *feeling* your anxiety rather than thinking your anxiety, it's important to remember that everything is temporary. Emotions, like anything else in life, don't last forever. They have a life cycle, and then they are done.

However, the one thing that can perpetuate an emotion is thinking about it. You can probably recall a time in your past when you felt sad, for example. Now, I don't want you to *do* this, but imagine if you had started thinking a lot about that time. You ruminated over the situation and the events involved. You listened to the music you listened to back then, and it brought up those feelings, and you got out photos that reminded you of those times. Do you think you'd start feeling down? You bet.

But if we let ourselves fully feel the emotion in the moment, stay present with that experience from the place within us of the neutral witness, and refrain from engaging with thoughts about it, it eventually eases up. I've seen this in my own life and over and over again with my clients. Remaining consciously and kindly present with the anxiety works.

The Wave of Emotion

Anxiety, like any emotion, is similar to a wave. Imagine yourself at a beach sitting and looking at the waves rolling in onto the sand.

First, a wave begins to build. The water surges and rises up, eventually becoming a crest. As it comes to the peak of its crest— that curling over into what we think of as the classic wave—it crashes into itself and rolls up onto the sand. It's foamy and white, flows on the shore, and then, having spent its energy, the water gently slides back and dissolves into the ocean again.

Have you ever gone swimming or bodysurfing at the beach? If you have, then you probably know not to turn your back on the waves. A wave that takes you unexpectedly can really pummel you; same thing if you stand there just looking at the wave as it comes at you. It can come down on you and toss you around intensely. I remember almost losing my breath a couple times as a child when I wasn't paying attention.

So how do you swim in the waves without getting pummeled? You watch them, position yourself, and when they come up on you, you dive in! You do the very thing that seems crazy when you're first learning to swim in the surf. I was terrified the first time I tried it. I thought it would be much worse to dive in, but I saw other people doing it, and they told me that was the best way. And when I gathered the courage to dive in and came up triumphantly on the other side, totally fine, I was elated!

That's the difference between accepting your emotions as opposed to pushing them away, pretending they aren't there, or judging yourself for having them. You're letting yourself get pummeled. So what we do instead is dive in—we let ourselves feel them as they pass through, and then we come up for air on the other side.

An Exercise in Feeling Your Anxiety

OK, you've probably been wondering, how do I do this, then? Here's a step by step process to feeling the anxiety, or any emotion you are experiencing, and allowing it to wash through you. Remember that at any time, if this process feels like too much, you can always choose to stop and take a break. Come back to it when you feel you're ready to dive in a little more. But if possible, allow yourself to explore beyond your comfort zone, and give the emotion time to complete its wave cycle.

Sit comfortably in a chair, preferably with your feet flat on the floor, but in a position that allows you to be both relaxed and alert. Close your eyes, and pay attention to your breath. Don't try to change anything about it yet; just notice the inhalations and exhalations.

Bring to mind something that causes you anxiety. Take a minute or so to remember the situation, the person, the words that were said, and any worries that arise while you think of it. Decide on the level of intensity of the anxiety on a scale from one to ten, one being complete calm and ten being a full-blown panic attack. Make note of that, and then turn inward again to your experience.

Next, shift your attention from the source of the anxiety to noticing your breath once more. What is happening with your inhalation? Is it long or short, deep or shallow, pleasant or unpleasant? Do you feel you are receiving enough air, or does it feel like it's not sufficient and takes a lot of effort to inhale? Notice anything you can about the inhalation as you are feeling this emotion of anxiety.

Do the same with the exhalation. Is it smooth or choppy? Does the outbreath feel complete—did you let all the air release? Or is there a tendency to hold onto it? Is it short or long, pleasant or unpleasant? Notice how the exhalation is affected by the experience of anxiety.

After your breath awareness, turn your attention to your overall body sensations. When you find the mind kicking in and wanting to tell stories about the anxiety, thank your mind, and then return to noticing the physical sensations. Where do you feel anxiety in your body? Check in with your forehead, eyes, jaw, neck, shoulders, hands, chest, back, belly, and legs. The sensations are unique to you and could be somewhere else. Are you feeling pain somewhere? Is there tension or a sense of agitation? Sometimes, people with anxiety have an overall restlessness, a feeling of energy moving around, or heat moving through the body. Notice what your sensations are in this experience of feeling fear, worry, or stress.

Be mindful of *how* you are noticing. This is not a practice in judging or being critical of yourself or the sensations. Let them be how they are. They are not good or bad, they are just how your body is feeling in this moment.

Try your best to be compassionate toward yourself during this experience of anxiety. Hold yourself gently in understanding that your body is suffering right now. Open your heart to this experience; feel it as fully as you can, with love and care for the parts of you that are suffering. Remember to practice *maitri*, being a good friend to yourself. You can witness

the sensations while practicing self-compassion for the
pain you feel.

Stay present with it. Breathe, deepening your inhalations and
lengthening your exhalations. People with anxiety often tend
to shorten their exhalation, so see if you can lengthen the
outbreath. Remember, this helps with relaxing the nervous
system. Be with the sensations, whether you are clenching
your teeth, furrowing your forehead, or perhaps feeling a
clutching in your stomach. Wherever the sensations are, stay
with them the way you would stay with a dear friend who
feels similarly.

Notice that the anxiety does not remain the same the whole
time. At some moments, it will feel more intense; at others,
less intense. Notice the ebbs and flows. And observe that
you have the capacity to ride those waves, to feel the crests
and falls of the experience of your anxiety, and that it really
does change.

Try to give yourself ten to thirty minutes of being present with
the physical experience of anxiety. Do your best to fully feel
it and give your attention to it. You may have to kindly shift
yourself away from *thinking* the anxiety back to *feeling* the
anxiety many, many times. That's OK, and very normal, but
you'll get better at staying with the feeling with some practice.
Set a timer if you find it helpful to know that you have a set
period of time for this exercise.

When you are nearing the end, allow a few minutes to find
your center within. Feel it in your belly, and then extend that
through your core. Add in your grounding, sending roots
down into the earth and deeply anchoring there. Remember
to also fill out your energy field and define your edge,
especially if you need to be around people soon afterwards.

This will help to stabilize you at the end of any kind of inner
work and prepares you for returning to your day or evening.

After that ten to thirty minute period, check in with yourself.
What are you feeling now? What sensations are in your body?
How is your breath? Are you still feeling your anxiety? If so,
where is it on the scale from one to ten? Chances are good
that it is lower than it was when you started. Simply by being
compassionately present with your anxiety, you can experience
the movement of the wave of emotion through you and then
release it. Sometimes, people can completely release their anxiety
through this exercise.

But if it's still there, that's OK. You probably learned a lot about
your anxiety through observing your breath, your sensations,
and the tendency to want to *think* it rather than *feel* it. That's
progress! And it will prepare you for the next important step:
listening to your anxiety.

Chapter 14

Listening to Your Anxiety

"When you talk, you are only repeating what you know. But if you listen, you may learn something new."

—The Dalai Lama

You've developed presence and embodiment in order to *feel* your anxiety and learned to hold it with self-compassion. Now, you're ready to *listen to* your anxiety.

Anxiety has a message for you, if you take the time to listen and receive it. It actually wants to be your helper, letting you know what needs tending to in your life. In fact, renaming anxiety as your helper or protector is a lot less negative and can change your perspective on your fears. It certainly is more pleasant to think of listening to your helper than listening to your anxiety, isn't it?

Learning to Listen

What are the components of listening? We have already covered many of them. The first is presence, which we explored in Chapter 9. You know what it's like to have a friend who is really, truly present with you when you talk. They make eye contact, give you their full attention, and don't let distractions like text messages or emails take precedence. You are their focus, and you know that you matter to them.

In order to listen to your anxiety (your helper!), you'll need to set aside your phone, the computer, your roommates or family members, and, of course, your work. This part of yourself needs

to get that it matters to you, enough for you to put all else aside
to attend to it. Then, it will reveal its secrets to you.

Secondly, when we listen, it's important to have an open heart.
We're open and receptive to what is being shared with us. This
is again the yogic concept of *maitri*, friendliness. We don't judge
what the anxiety has to say; we listen with an open mind, even if
it's a bit uncomfortable to hear.

Lastly, good listening shows that we care. Treat the feelings of
worry and fear with the caring attitude of a good friend who
is intent on finding some way to be helpful. This is where we
apply *karuna*, compassion, to ourselves in the listening process.
Love that part of yourself and hold it with tenderness. Have
an attitude and energy of unconditional love for all aspects of
yourself—even the anxiety.

As you "listen," keep in mind that it isn't just with our ears—
albeit our inner ears—that we're listening. We listen with our
inner eyes to see what colors, shapes, symbols, and images might
arise. We listen with our body to all the sensations that we notice,
as well as with the sense of touch: textures, density, and so on. If
you could hold the anxiety in your hands, what would it feel like?
How heavy or light would it be? Would it be hard, or squishy like
a soft ball? Of course, we listen to words, sounds, and vibrations.
Through listening with the heart, we attend to the rise and fall of
emotions and new feeling states emerging. We're listening with
our intuition, our gut, and our soul. Listening expands into a
whole body, whole being experience.

Trust What You Receive

While developing the skill to deeply listen to the anxiety (or the ability to listen to any emotion or aspect of your inner self), do not discount anything that arises. Even the most seemingly insignificant thought, word, sensation, memory, or image can have meaning. You may believe that it was just random or that you got distracted while you were listening. Don't believe those thoughts. Make a note of it anyway. It may end up being nothing, but it just as easily could be the key to shifting the whole fear dynamic for you.

Trust what you receive. You are tapping into a different part of yourself than your conscious mind, and as you deepen in this practice, you can access your Higher Self, the wise, loving, transcendent, and yes, *calm* part of you! Even your spirit guides, angels, or the Divine itself may be able to communicate to you through the anxiety if you give it a chance.

Case Study: Learning to Let Go

Marcus was a successful architect who started at his company fresh out of college and worked his way up to a position as a senior manager in charge of his branch. He was responsible for overseeing several projects a month, as well as managing over twenty employees. Back at home, Marcus was a father of two girls and had a loving wife. Life was good, but he was still stressed and anxious.

He found me through yoga classes and then came in for sessions to work on his stress. His body was always tense; when he sat down, he had perfect yoga posture—too perfect. You could see him holding it all together in the neck, shoulders, torso, and down his arms into his hands, which were a bit rigid. Although he could breathe deeply, it was forced, like he was trying to do it "right" and holding his body in position carefully. His jaw was clenched. Stress coursed through his body.

I invited Marcus to sit with his eyes closed and begin to feel his body. It became clear to him that he was feeling fear. As he explored the sensations, I guided him in discerning what message the fear had for him. He felt like his heart and chest were pushed up into his collar bones, and there was a sensation of stuckness all through his upper torso. I suggested he focus his attention in his heart area, breathe into it, and listen.

Tears began to trickle silently down his cheeks while he attended to listening to his heart. And then he shared what he heard: "You need to listen to me more. I can help you." He realized that he hadn't been paying much attention to his heart—he's always trying to fix everything, keep it all together, and move on to the next thing, not stopping to feel what is actually happening within him. Over a few sessions, as he continued to deepen his skill at listening to his heart, Marcus' body softened. He recognized that he didn't need to fix himself; his body sensations as he sat with the tension and stress again and again let him know that he is supported, right here in this moment, just as he is. As he opened his heart and his body, he realized that he just needed to open to allow that support and his anxiety dissipated.

An Exercise for Listening to Your Anxiety

Let's try a listening exercise with your anxiety. Set aside fifteen to thirty minutes for this, although over time you can learn to do the process more quickly. It will begin with the "Feeling Your Anxiety" practice and then go deeper within. Allow yourself to feel the anxiety within you, and you will notice it reflected through the body.

I like to start with how anxiety is reflected in the breath. Be present with the inhalations and exhalations. Then, focus on the inhalation as you did before. What sensations do you notice? Let's say that you notice the inhalation is choppy and that it's difficult to get a full breath. You also notice that you're breathing into your upper chest but can't seem to expand it down into the belly.

Now, you can ask the anxiety what it is revealing to you through the inhalation. Remember, the anxiety is trying to help you, so open to hearing its message through your breath. You can be still and listen, paying attention to any thoughts, words, sounds, images, feelings, and textures. For example, you might imagine that the feeling in your chest is a heavy weight sitting on top of your rib cage, making it hard to breathe in. You might literally see it there, a black, metallic, heavy weight.

Continue "listening." Maybe some words emerge; perhaps in this case, you may hear the words, "It's so heavy." You could inquire—what feels heavy in my life? Ah, a response might arise; the weight of my family, my family is weighing on me.

Ask more questions. What about my family is weighing on me? An answer may arise spontaneously; all the negative energy from my father is coming down on me, and I bear it for my whole family. A scene may unfold in your mind's eye of a time in your childhood when your father blamed you for something bad that happened in the family, and you may again feel all the shame you felt then, like a weight on your chest.

Now, what do you want to ask the anxiety about this? You might want to ask, "What does the weight want to tell me now?" Listen. Or you may ask your heart how it feels about this heaviness: what would your heart like? What would help your heart to release this heaviness?

As you listen, you may hear answers, such as: "This weight was never about you—it was about your father feeling helpless," "I don't want this weight on my heart anymore!" "Love yourself more," or the little girl in you may ask for you to hold her and let her know it's not her fault. Your little girl (or boy) inside may want your love and reassurance that she is OK and that her father is not here and no longer has power over her. Listen to whatever arises in your own heart or whatever sensations you notice, especially during the inhalation.

Let any emotions that arise wash through, as in the wave process we explored in the last chapter. And then check in again with your breath and with the experience of the anxiety. Can you breathe more smoothly and more deeply? Do you feel less anxiety? You can also do the same process listening to the exhale or any other sensation in the body.

Remember to complete your "Listening to Your Anxiety" practice with centering, grounding, and defining your energetic space before you open your eyes and return to your regular activities, even if you do this right before bed.

You may want to have a friend help you through this process, or work with a therapist who has a holistic, somatic, or body/mind orientation to their work, especially if you find this challenging or too uncomfortable. In both my individual sessions and my course based on this book, I assist my students in developing skill in listening to their anxiety, as it is pivotal in transforming fear into deep healing. Then, you'll be able to do it anytime and almost anywhere when you have a few minutes to be present with yourself.

Ways to Process

After you have received the messages, wisdom, and healing from listening to your anxiety, take some time to process what happened. Your "helper" may reveal even more to you after doing the practice. This will deepen the transformation and support you in more lasting transformation of your fears and worries.

Here are some possible ways you can process, and you may think of some of your own, too:

· *Journaling*—write down the insights, guidance, and answers you receive. I strongly recommend keeping a journal to capture your experiences and wisdom that you can return to again and again; use it to reflect on and help you through other times of anxiety.

· *Art*—draw, paint, sculpt, or make collages about the experience.

· *Write a Song or a Poem*—hum a tune that fits with the process or matches the energy of your transformation; create a poem that embodies what your anxiety revealed and how you changed.

· *Dreamwork*—pay attention to your dreams after doing a "Listening to Your Anxiety" exercise. Write them down and reflect on their further messages.

· *Dance*—move and dance out the anxiety and your new way of being or feeling.

· *Write a Letter* to Your Anxiety, or let the anxiety write a letter to you expressing what it wants to tell you and how it wants you to change or grow.

· *Step Out in Nature*—take a walk down the street, a saunter through a garden, or a hike in the woods. Notice what captures your attention around you; perhaps a boulder, a flower, or a dead log, for example. Have a conversation with that part of nature—what does it want to communicate to you about your anxiety?

Can you think of others? Send them to me at Connie@ AwakeningSelf.com!

The more you practice listening to your anxiety, not only will you become more proficient at understanding the messages it wants to communicate, but you'll be able to move through the practice more quickly. Sometimes, I am able to move completely through a feeling of being overwhelmed and return to feeling ease in just a few minutes. Other times, it takes me a few days of exploration and processing. It may not always happen that easily, but eventually you will be able to shift out of anxiety-producing thoughts and events, gain clarity and insight, and find your inner calm again.

Chapter 15

Empowering Action

"The issue of spiritual power is to meet the limited mortal circumstance with unlimited thought."

—Marianne Williamson

You've come a long way, my friend! If you've reached this point of the book, then you have developed a bit of presence, embodiment, and self-compassion. You have an understanding—and hopefully some practice—with feeling your anxiety and listening to its messages. Now, you're ready to deepen into the journey that fear is intended to catalyze.

You see, anxiety is the initiator: it is creating an initiation into a more empowered way of being. From a spiritual perspective, the anxiety, worry, and fears have arisen to take you to the next level of your journey.

It's like leveling up in a video game, a wonderful metaphor that my friend and intuitive coach, Stacey J. Warner (www. staceyjwarner.com), likes to use. When you complete one level and move up to the next one, it's like starting all over again. Everything is more challenging. In life, that can seem pretty intimidating and can bring up anxiety all over again. But it means that you're expanding into a greater expression of your true essence.

The Two Kinds of Fear: Known and Unknown

The definition of fear is "an unpleasant emotion caused by the belief that someone or something is dangerous, likely to cause pain, or a threat." I find this definition very helpful because it distinguishes actual threat (which would be true danger of harm) from *the belief* that something could be dangerous. As we explored in the introduction, anxiety is essentially a repetitive state of fear, a state of awareness focused on what *could* be cause for fear. We perpetuate the belief that something could be dangerous, and that arouses a state of anxiety.

There are, in fact, two kinds of fear: fear of the known and fear of the unknown.

The first kind of fear goes back to our cave-person days. It's fear based on survival. If you are really being chased down by a lion or a great white shark, you *know* you have something to be afraid of, don't you? So fear kicks in our fight-or-flight response, and we hightail it out of the savannah or the water. It gives us that extra boost to initiate the action we need to take to get out of danger and into safety.

The other kind of fear is fear of the unknown. It is distinct, but sneaky. It causes physiological responses similar to those induced by the fear of the known. We feel the muscles tensing, the stomach knotting up, or the forehead wrinkling. The heart rate increases, and we may sweat a bit or shake. Perhaps we don't manifest these obvious signs, but it can be more subtle. There's just a restlessness, an inability to stay still; the thoughts race, and we want to do something, anything, just to feel better. These symptoms and more are what many people experience as anxiety.

This fear is based on the mystery, the unknown, the unpredictability of existence. There's no immediate threat to our lives. Probably no one is trying to hurt us or shame us. But we imagine that they are or could be. We believe that if we try this new thing or step out of our comfort zone, we'll come to harm.

On an even deeper level, we often feel this second kind of fear when we're leveling up, especially on the path of personal and spiritual growth. We're evolving and expanding into new awareness and trying out more fulfilling and empowered ways of being in the world. As we're changing, even in positive ways, fear is likely to rear its head. It's unfamiliar and uncomfortable, and that sets off our danger alarms—even if the danger is solely in our own imagination.

Fear Indicates the Onset of Power

This fear or anxiety about the unknown indicates the *onset of power*. When fear arises and you don't see any immediate threat, but you acknowledge that you are imagining it, you can bet that some part of you knows the game is up. Your inner self recognizes that you have been limited—playing small. It's giving you the nudge you need; fear is waking you up. Now, you get to play at a higher level.

Something powerful is happening in your life. That's why you feel fearful. It's actually calling you to step into your power in a new way. The fear and anxiety are letting you know that you're not willing to simply settle for how it is or how you've been in the past. You know that you want to awaken more deeply or express yourself more fully. When that begins to happen for you, and you're getting a taste of what's possible, sometimes that anxiety kicks in. It doesn't want you to leave the zone of the familiar— that's unknown territory! And we believe that the unknown is dangerous, because we can't control it.

Your Empowering Action

When our anxiety is unfounded on anything in reality at this time and is focused on what *could* happen, it's time to listen to our anxiety and discover our *empowering action*. When fear arises, it has a call to greatness hidden within it. Or if that word is too intimidating or boastful for you, think of it as simply a call to be something greater than you've allowed yourself to be—to be a higher expression of your true self.

This empowering action practice is similar to what is referred to as "opposite action" in Dialectical Behavior Therapy, a counseling approach that integrates aspects of mindfulness, interpersonal skills, distress tolerance, and emotional regulation. With opposite action, the client identifies the emotion they are experiencing, reflects on whether the emotion is an appropriate response to the situation, recognizes what the emotion makes them feels like doing, and then chooses an action that is the opposite of that.

For example, if you feel like curling up in a ball from fear, it may not be a helpful response to what is happening. Let's say you have social anxiety and must speak in front of a group. Curling up in a ball wouldn't be the best way to deal with the fear, would it? So the opposite action might be to jump up and volunteer to speak.

Empowering action is a bit different. Opposite action may be helpful, but it may not always be the best response either. Empowering action comes from a deeper exploration of the emotion and discernment as to what will transform the situation and the emotions. It comes from intently listening to what the fear is expressing and the needs it signals, then discovering what would both honor the feeling and take you a step toward how you want to feel—more calm, confident, and courageous.

Case Study: Social Anxiety

Farima is a woman in her forties who has worked in the tech industry for many years, coding software and managing small teams overseas. Although she did have leadership experience, it had mostly been online, not in person. In face-to-face social situations, she struggled with opening up and being vulnerable with people. Her social anxiety left her feeling disconnected. She sought out my women's retreats to help her relax, feel connected to others, and begin to open up more.

While we were having a group discussion, she realized that she feared the judgment of others about a situation in her life. She was reticent to reveal it to others, but we did a process that allowed her to feel the anxiety and listen to it. She decided to speak up and share it.

This wasn't just doing the opposite of what she felt like doing, which was to clam up and shut down. She discerned that in some situations, it wouldn't be appropriate to share it solely because it would be the opposite of her impulse. Her anxiety taught her that it might not always be wise to speak her thoughts but that she can trust her intuition to discern who is safe to express herself with. Her body felt relaxed in that moment with the supportive

women, so she spoke her truth and was met with appreciation
for sharing her experience and compassionate understanding.
This created an opening in her heart and her body, and the
anxiety softened.

When you spend time *listening to your anxiety*, ask it this
question: what empowering action does your anxiety want you
to take? If we just remain in the fear and allow it to run our life,
we stay small. To find the empowering action needed in the
situation, we probe a bit deeper.

Asking the Questions of Fear

Now, we will take the "Listening to Your Anxiety" practice a little
deeper. Let's find out what your fear wants and how you can
become empowered by it.

Here are some helpful questions to ask the fear. I encourage you
to get out a journal and write down the answers you receive.
I also recommend a drawing pad and some art materials so
you can express what you receive in a nonverbal way (i.e.,
beyond words). Again, don't discount anything. Just wait to see
what comes.

Begin as always by closing your eyes and taking some deep,
mindful breaths. Become present in this moment, and practice
the skills of embodiment: center, ground, and fill out to your
energetic edge.

Feel the anxiety in your body. As you feel and listen to it, ask
these questions and write your responses:

· What are you trying to protect me from?

· What would be a more effective way of protecting me than this fear?

· What action would you like for me to take?

· What would be the most empowering action for me to take that would allow this fear to release?

· What are the baby steps to being able to take that action?

Trust whatever arises in response to your questions. If you have other questions that arise, go ahead and explore them with your fears. If you aren't getting any words or thoughts, but you're seeing images, colors, symbols, or feeling sensations or a desire to move, write them down, draw them on your drawing pad, or get up on your feet and let your body express itself.

Let these thoughts, images, and movements percolate within you. Continue to journal about this for the next few days, and see what arises on the paper and in your life. Opportunities to take empowering actions will likely appear around you, and messages how to do that will, too, if you are on the lookout for them! I'd love to hear your experiences and answer your questions—send them to me at Connie@AwakeningSelf.com.

An Unexpected Empowering Action

At times, the best action to take to transform your anxiety is no action at all! Fear usually wants us to run, hide, and get the heck out of wherever we are. But it may be more empowering to stand your ground.

By taking a stand, right here, even in the midst of the anxiety, you demonstrate that fear is powerless over you. It can't make you do anything. You can be still and wait. Wait for what, you might say?

The Taoists have an answer. Taoism is an ancient, earth-based religion from China that recognizes the Divine manifest in everything in nature; they call it the *Tao*, which has no precise translation. It's the unnamable, infinite presence that is the source of All That Is.

In Taoism, you might be encouraged to practice *wu wei*. This is *the action that arises of itself*. We let go of our compulsion to do something, take some time to just be, and allow something to arise for us. This is the wisdom and power of *waiting*: sometimes, no action is better. Taking action can stir everything up unnecessarily, especially when we act out of fear. We can pause, wait, and allow the Universe to show the way.

The unexpected power of not-acting is that it is an affirmation of trust that the Universe has all the wisdom and intelligence needed to shift us out of fear and into freedom. It will lead us to the most empowering action without forcing it to happen. As we let go and trust that guidance to arise, it will.

Take a Stand (or Strike a Pose)

You might not know in your mind what needs to be done to step out of fear and into your power, but *your body* might. As you tune into the anxiety in your body and ask again what empowering action it wishes for you to take, feel how your body wants to move.

Stand comfortably and take some relaxing breaths. Feel your body as you're standing, and notice what impulses you have. If you could move your body in any way, how would you want to move right now? Allow it to happen. Let your body make those movements spontaneously. Do not try to figure out what you're "supposed" to do. Shoulds, have-tos, musts, and supposed-tos are generally not empowering and usually arise from fear. Instead, allow your body to express itself. Dance, shake, shimmy, crawl, or jump the fear out and the courage in!

Then, strike a pose that embodies your newfound way of being. Take that stance. Feel what it is like in your body. You are taking a stand for your own transformation. How do your feet and legs want to be positioned? Which way are you facing, and where are you looking? What do your arms want to do?

Feel what it is like to take this stance. What do you want to say as you hold this pose? Describe the energy you feel. Think of words that might describe your experience—strong, flexible, fluid, flowing, direct, supple, clear, calm, serene, undisturbed?

Finally, tune in to *who* you are being called to *be* in this stance. What qualities long to emerge from within you? Determination, trust, intuition, leadership, compassion, service...notice what qualities arise, qualities that the fear is

actually beckoning to come forth from within you. Speak the
words aloud, write them in your journal, or let colors and forms
express the experience on your drawing pad.

The Upper Limit Problem

There is another time when fear of the unknown can show up in
our lives: when things are going well. In fact, we can have anxiety
about positive feelings and experiences, too. This is common on
the spiritual path. We might be having deeper, more profound
meditations or feeling an expanded experience of love welling
up within us. And then we may freak out, because it's such
unfamiliar territory, and create anxiety to pull us out of it!

This can show up as worrying about how long this good feeling
will last and wondering when it will end—and then it does. We
might fear losing our sense of self (with the ego clinging to its
perception of control over your life) as we expand into more
refined states of meditation and may suddenly decide to stop
meditating. The feeling of love flowing within might overwhelm
us, and then we may cut it off because we worry that others think
we're weird for being so joyous.

Gay Hendricks, renowned motivational speaker and author of
the bestselling book, *The Big Leap*, calls this the *Upper Limit
Problem*. He noticed it happening in his own life: "I have a
limited tolerance for feeling good. When I hit my Upper Limit, I
manufacture thoughts that make me feel bad...or do something
else that brings me back down within the bounds of my
limited tolerance."

It's common to feel fear of creating the big, positive changes we
want in our lives. Anxiety often shows up when we've made the

leap into that new, exciting, transformative life. Sometimes, it just seems too good to be true; when is the other shoe going to drop? That's when we may undermine our own growth and fall into the *Upper Limit Problem.*

Hendricks says that the solution to the Upper Limit Problem—and the anxiety that accompanies it—is *to increase our willingness to feel good* inside and to have our lives go well. It seems ridiculous: why wouldn't we want our lives to go well? But we may have a subtle attachment to the dramas of sadness, worry, fear, anxiety, and struggle. We may believe that it isn't possible to live life without them. But Hendricks asserts that it is.

Changing Our Perspective Empowers Us

One way to increase the amount of time that we feel good every day is to change our perspective about our anxiety. I've been working with you throughout this book to help you see and respond to your anxiety in new ways. Now, by looking at it as a harbinger of empowerment, you can redefine your anxiety.

There are many acronyms for fear that help us change our perspective about it, but one that I first learned of recently has been credited to Neale Donald Walsh, author of *Conversations with God.* He says that when we feel fear or anxiety, we can redefine it as **f**eeling **e**xcited **a**nd **r**eady. If you think about it, this is true. Fear and excitement have almost the exact same physiological response. This readies our body for whatever is required of it, such as the need to run or fight.

We can choose to see our lives as bringing anxiety-provoking situations, or instead see life as bringing adventure and positive transformation. My dear friend Tim Custis (timcustis.com), spiritual mentor and creator of Spiral Release Bodywork®, says, "When we feel a sense of adventure, taking action is much easier because we want to move forward. Our fear shifts or drops away entirely and no longer is an obstacle, and it becomes a motivator... From this new perspective, you can start taking action instead of being paralyzed in a fearful story of your own making."

Taking Your Empowering Action—in Baby Steps

You may not yet have a sense of an empowering action to take in response to your excitement (i.e., anxiety) about what lies ahead of you. But if you do, it's time to consider stepping out into that new way of being—baby style.

When we learn to walk, we actually don't walk; first, we crawl. That accustoms us to the experience of getting around on our own with more stability. Four limbs on the ground are easier to balance on than two! This is like doing our dance, our movements, our journaling, and our drawings of the messages and actions called forth from the fear. It prepares us to step out into the world.

Then, we learn to stand up. It's a very exciting moment in a toddler's life. They see and feel things differently on two feet. Taking your stand is the grown-up version of this. You learn to embody the new qualities and characteristics called forth from anxiety.

But you still don't walk yet! A toddler then learns to cruise, stepping about with the assistance of a couch, table, or chair to hold onto. Remember when you first went to a skating rink? Like me, you might have held onto the rails all the way around the rink, trying to adjust to the new balance on the blades or wheels. That's cruising. And that's your next empowering action.

Practice embodying the new actions or qualities amongst those you love, the people you feel safe with. They're like the sturdy rails you hold onto while you're trying to find your new balance. Tell them what your endeavor is. Choose people you trust who can support your vision for living with confidence, courage, and calm, even in the face of the unknown. Have them help you reframe your fears into adventures or ways that you can expand beyond your self-imposed limitations.

If you don't have someone like that in your life, tap into your own Higher Self, the part of you that is all-knowing, wise, kind, loving, powerful, compassionate, supportive—all the qualities you'd like to embody. Your Higher Self *is* that. Imagine having a conversation with your Higher Self, and ask her to help you reframe your fears and see life in a new perspective. Write down your dialogues, or speak them into a recorder. Play it for yourself when you need support and encouragement. Your Higher Self can hold your hand while you skate around your rink of life.

Then, time to take your baby steps! This is where you let go of the rails and walk on your own. But babies don't take huge strides. They take one small step at a time.

What little step are you willing and able to take into empowered action? What small change can you implement? What quality would you like to put into practice? What is the first part of the adventure you'd like to embark upon? You're now ready not only to release your anxiety, but to experience confident, joyful living and inner peace.

Chapter 16

Surrender

"Sticking with that uncertainty, getting the knack of relaxing in the midst of chaos, learning not to panic— this is the spiritual path."

—Pema Chodron

After reading the "Empowering Action" chapter, you might wonder: what is beyond empowering action? Well, this next key is the biggest step yet in transforming your anxiety into a catapult for your spiritual growth. This is the practice of surrender.

I know the word surrender sounds scary. You may be thinking, "Weren't you going to help me with my anxiety, not create more of it?" I totally understand. Surrender sounds like a frightening and disempowering thing to do. Doesn't that mean just giving up?

Not at all. At least, not in the way you're thinking. Let's take some deep breaths together. Really, this is such a beautiful step, it has made the most impact for me of anything I have done to release my own fears as well as for my spiritual awakening process. It can for you, too. So let's walk together, gently and slowly, through what I mean about surrender, and let's discover how it is the doorway to your freedom within.

What Do You Mean by Surrender?

First of all, it's important for you to understand where I'm coming from. This is a spiritual surrender, which is a key aspect of the mystical paths of most of the religions of the world. It will not disempower you; in fact, it is the greatest empowering action you can take in response to anxiety. But we don't take this step lightly. A solid spiritual foundation and the other components of overcoming your anxiety that have been outlined in this book are essential for the practice of surrender to be fruitful.

When we think of surrender, we often think of conceding— like losing a battle, right? You raise the white flag and call out, "Uncle! Enough already! I give up!" That's the classic understanding of surrender: giving in to the more powerful force.

In a way, that's exactly what I'm talking about here; more on that in a moment.

So if surrender is losing the battle, then let's think about that— what kind of battle has been going on? Because it's not an outer battle we're discussing here. You're not in a battle with the things you fear, nor trying to go out and conquer them. If you were and if you were successful at that, you wouldn't have picked up this book. We try to fight our anxiety, but that usually doesn't get us very far, because, as we know, "what we resist, persists." That kind of aggression, even toward something seemingly outside of us, usually ends up turned back on us; we end up attacking ourselves whenever we lose.

The battle here in this quest to transform our anxiety is inside our own minds. We are battling with ourselves, and that is causing all kinds of suffering. Our minds are in a constant struggle between aspects of ourselves, whether it's the fearful part, the courageous part, the logical part, the part of ourselves that wants to push through everything, or some other. It's exhausting, frustrating, and just perpetuates more struggle.

Surrender Brings Serenity

Wouldn't it be nice to just lay down all the arms and end the battle? Surrender brings serenity. What we're looking for is *not* to stop all the things out there that cause us to be fearful. I suggest letting go of the idea of shutting down the part of you that gets scared. That's a very human reaction, and it's probably coming from a very young, innocent child part of you. That child within needs you to love and care for it, not try to make it go away.

When we stop fighting with and attacking ourselves, we can then feel serenity inside instead of increasing anxiety. This is the first aspect of surrender. When we see the inner struggle going on, and notice the different sides battling for control of our psyche, we can step out of the battle and surrender. We can step into the neutral witness for a bit and decide that there's no right or wrong, there's nothing we have to do, in this moment. We can simply surrender it all.

The Process of Surrender

So what does that look like? What is the surrender process?

We begin the process of surrender by looking at the ego. The ego, or sense of self (I, me, and mine), which we often associate with our personality, wants to run the show. It wants to feel important, powerful, and in charge. This means that it must be in control. The ego believes that everything should be under its control, not just inside of us, but outside of us as well.

Anxiety is very difficult for the ego. It's disturbed by anxiety, because there's a perception that something out there is out of its control, and it doesn't like that one bit! So what does it do? The ego goes full force into trying to get everything under its command. This can be really crazy-making, because honestly there are a lot of things out there that aren't within our control. I know, it sucks, but that is just how it is. We can try to create our reality all we want, but there will still be things that just *happen*.

Naturally, if the ego believes everything should be under its control, and then there are things that aren't, it will interpret those things as something to be afraid of. It will go hog wild attempting to control what it can't, and guess what happens to your level of anxiety? Yep, it will get worse. There's nothing like trying to control the uncontrollable to exacerbate fears and worries. All that focus on manhandling everything will also create obsessive, anxiety-based thoughts and perceptions. It's a vicious cycle.

Surrendering the Thoughts

The process of surrender involves letting go of our thoughts. Most of the time, we cling to them like prized possessions. This means that we believe them.

You may think, well, they're my thoughts, of course I believe them! But thoughts aren't reality. In the chapter "Feeling Your Anxiety," you recognized that thoughts interfere with actually feeling our emotions and definitely hinder the ability of an emotion to complete its cycle.

But you probably also have discovered—or will now—that thoughts aren't real. They are simply impulses that go through your awareness. Many of them are based on what is called *sam-ska-ras* in yogic philosophy. These are latent tendencies or very old habits that not only go back through this lifetime but can accompany you through many lifetimes. They're like deer trails etched into the hillside of your mind.

The habitual thoughts (and associated emotions) pop up over and over until there's a well-worn trail, and that is the conditioned latent tendency, or *samskara*. The idea of going off-trail seems like a big deal that would require heavy-duty clothing, machetes, and a lot of sweat. And that's not far from the truth.

Real surrender involves giving up the thought patterns that keep you stuck in the anxiety. We may have a thought that speaking in public is scary—after all, it is the number one fear people have besides death! But is that true? If it's true, we'd be able to prove it for certain. The reality is that it may make us tremble, it may not go perfectly, but we can probably speak before an audience and survive, and even avoid having any tomatoes thrown at us. It's our thoughts, not reality, that tell us it's life-threatening.

Thoughts are the impulses of that old conditioning. But they are not real or true in themselves. The thought that "this chair is brown" is just a thought. The chair may be brown, but the *thought* isn't the reality of the chair or its brownness. It's just the way our mind wants to describe the experience. The actual essence of the chair is beyond the words we use to describe it or the color we have labeled it with.

We can surrender our thoughts to the Divine. For each thought that comes up—especially those anxiety-producing ones—we can examine it and recognize that hey, this is just a thought. It's not real. I don't have to believe it. I can surrender this now and be open to something else, maybe even to calm serenity.

Everything we have done up to this point will help you transform and release anxiety when it arises. Now, with surrender, we can not only alleviate it as it forms—we can pull up the roots of it from its source. We can surrender the thought forms, control, and our personal sense of self to something greater than us.

Ishvara Pranidhana

Enter yoga philosophy to guide us in this practice of surrender. In yoga philosophy, this is known as *Ishvara Pranidhana* (pronounced EESH-vah-rah prah-nee-DAH-nuh). *Ishvara* translates as "the supreme being," also known as God or Spirit; I like to use the words, "the Divine." *Pranidhana* is devotional dedication or surrender of the self. Put together, they signify "Surrender to the Divine." This surrendering of ourselves to the Divine—that which is beyond all of us—is what I mentioned earlier about surrendering to a more powerful, transcendent force.

What can you surrender to that is bigger than you? Consider your beliefs. Since you're on a spiritual path, you probably have something that you believe in. What is the higher power in your life? You might call it God or Goddess, Jesus, Buddha, Mohammed, Jehovah, Shiva, Krishna, or Shakti, or it may be Nature, the Source, or the Universe that is your higher power or the Divine to you. Even if none of those speaks to you—even if you were, say, an atheist—there is still something bigger than you, a higher principle that you deeply believe in. Choose Love, Peace, Consciousness, or Truth.

This is what you surrender to when you practice *Ishvara Pranidhana*. You're not surrendering to a person or even a thing. You're surrendering to an energy and presence that is infinitely larger than your personal self. Here is the opportunity to allow something far beyond you to support and guide your life.

My Self-Surrender on the Plane

I had a palpable experience of self-surrender on a flight I took from the East Coast back to my home in California. The flight was pretty smooth for the first part, but then we started to hit some bumps. Turbulence had been a trigger for my anxiety ever since my daughter was born, and I had done a lot of work on releasing my fears. But when the ride became bumpy, the same worry and agitation arose. My palms broke out in a cold sweat, my body became tense, and my thoughts were fearful. I had been through this many times before and did my breathing techniques and grounding...much of what I've covered in this book. It improved, but just wouldn't let go.

Then I realized: perhaps *I* need to let go. What if I surrendered myself fully to the turbulence? What if I just allowed myself to be with it, to feel it as a manifestation of the Divine? After all, everything in the universe arises from that source. If I saw everything around me as an aspect of the Divine, wouldn't the turbulence be, too? And what would it be like if I allowed myself to become one with it?

I figured I had nothing to lose. No amount of my desire to stop it or control it was going to change the impact of the winds around the plane, and honestly, if I believed I could control it, then whenever it felt out of my control, that would be cause for sheer panic, because it shouldn't be! By letting go into it, I turned all of that on its head and allowed the Divine to express itself through the rough ride.

I did my best to relax into the seat and actually feel the shaking— to imagine myself as those gusts of wind and to flow around as if I were the air particles, the plane, the atmosphere in which it all played out. I felt myself connected to all of creation in that moment. As my concentration deepened and I allowed myself to feel the movements in my body, I noticed a peace permeating me: an ease, a bit of relaxation. I was elated! For a few minutes, the anxiety transformed into simply being with the turbulence as it was, rather than my trying to push it away and separate myself from the experience.

The anxiety did return after those blissful few minutes, but it lessened in intensity. Surrendering allowed me to experience Oneness, even in one of my most anxiety-provoking situations.

Surrender to Oneness

Surrendering to something greater allows us to let go of our sense of separation from Spirit, from All That Is. Rama Jyoti Vernon, cofounder of Yoga Journal magazine and author of *Patanjali's Yoga Sutras: Gateway to Enlightenment, Chapter One*, says, "*Ishvara* is not external. It is the internal core of being...the inner *guru* and companion of the soul. In the practice of *Ishvara Pranidhana*, the realization dawns that the Universal is already within us."

Here's the spiritual paradox: when you surrender to the Divine, you're not surrendering to something outside of yourself. You're allowing yourself to be One with that transcendent presence within you. It's already here, right inside, but our anxiety separates us from realizing it. The sense of a separate self—ego—keeps the fears out there, God out there, and ourselves in a lonely, frightening world.

Trust

The greatest challenge of surrender is trust. We must have supreme trust in that which we surrender ourselves to. That is why it is essential to consider what the Divine is to you and what you deeply trust.

When we have anxiety, it's difficult to trust, isn't it? Yet learning to trust is the backbone of being free from anxiety. You may be thinking, *I just can't trust. I don't really trust anything.*

But I bet you do.

I bet there are things that you trust in that you don't even think about. Do you trust that the sun will rise (even if behind clouds) tomorrow? How about spring—do you trust that it will come after winter? There are simple things in our day-to-day life, like trusting that the water will flow when we turn on a faucet, or that our key will fit in the ignition of our car. Right now, I bet you trust that your blood is circulating through your body. Of course, there may be rare exceptions, like if you had a blood disease, but generally most of us are trusting our bodies to do their thing. You could probably name a number of things, if you give it some thought, that you trust.

Since you're on a spiritual path, then there is something that has called you that you trust in. You sense that there is a presence bigger than you and that a more expanded state of consciousness is possible for you.

Put your trust in that; and trust that if you surrender to a greater consciousness and open yourself to it, something transformative will happen with your anxiety.

No Separation

The practice of surrender helps to heal our sense of separation. When we are fearful, we perceive a gaping chasm between us and the object of fear; it's me, and I'm entirely separate from that person over there, or that turbulence on the airplane, or that crowd in front of me. The constant perception of separation is the source of fear, the sense that "it's out there, and it could get me."

But what if we no longer saw that separation? What if we were able to not only see our connection with the object of fear but feel united with it? When we are united, there's nothing to fear.

Case Study: Surrender and the Trees

While I was teaching a yoga philosophy class as part of a yoga teacher training, Carla sat attentively. She was drawn to teach yoga as an adjunct and an alternative to a less-than-soul-satisfying career in real estate. Her eyes lit up in surprise when I introduced *Ishvara Pranidhana* and mentioned that even atheists can be spiritual. She had been raised Christian, but it didn't resonate with her anymore. It had never occurred to her before that spirituality, and her own higher power, didn't need to be religious.

Soon after, she contacted me to work together on her anxiety issues, and one day I took her on an Ecotherapy session, outdoors at a local park. Her heart and attention were drawn to the greenest, leafiest tree—it was alive, abundant, and vibrant, in contrast to the bare trees that had not yet received their early spring foliage. She lay down under its canopy, gazing up at the branches. "I want to be up there, where it's green and peaceful," she said. She felt grounded, calm, and relaxed and allowed herself to surrender to the support of the tree, the earth, the sky, and the peace that she felt.

We affirmed her experience in statements: "I am strong and stable. I open to receive abundance." Then, I encouraged her to take a closer look at one of the "bare" trees. To her surprise, there were buds all over it; it was full of life, but it just hadn't manifested it to our eyes yet. She received a message from this tree, too: "Trust the process of your growth. Don't be impatient." After this session, she felt safer in the world, knowing she had something bigger she could trust and be supported by.

Trust the Process

As Carla discovered, one of my favorite sayings that I attempt to live by, and which I encourage my students and clients to heed as well, is "Trust the process." Even if finding a higher power doesn't quite work for you, I find that trusting the process always does for me.

There is a Divine order in the universe. The planet knows how to rotate and travel around the sun. Seeds know how to grow into redwood trees or wheat. We can put our trust in whatever process is happening in our lives, including the experience of anxiety. This is not about surrendering to the circumstances or surrendering to our fears, but surrendering to the higher process of what those circumstances reveal, teach, or bring forth from within us.

There is a blessing in our anxiety. Our fears reveal the limited perceptions we have held onto and give us the opportunity to perceive new, expanded possibilities. Anxiety is the trigger that holds the key to our freedom. Let go, surrender, and trust that something greater is unfolding in your life, supporting you, and allowing you to live more in faith, harmony, and inner peace.

Part IV

Living a More Calm, Confident, and Courageous Life

Let's put it all together. You're ready to hit the road of life with your new skills that soften anxiety's grip and put you back in the driver seat. Keep in mind that you're going to encounter some bumps on the road. It's normal for anxiety to arise again. I'm preparing you for that, and for how to step beyond the stumbling blocks into a more expansive, courageous way to live. You're awakening from your anxiety, and you're ready to apply what you've learned. Step forward into living the keys and finding inner peace.

Chapter 17

Resistance to Resilience

*"Children, learn to be relaxed in all circumstances.
Whatever you do and wherever you are, relax and you
will see how powerful it is... Once you learn this art,
everything happens spontaneously and effortlessly."*

—Mata Amritanandamayi

It's not uncommon to arrive at this part of the book both excited
about the possibilities but also feeling some resistance to working
with these keys and letting go of anxiety. Even if we're clear that
being free of worry and overwhelm would be much better for us,
we tend to like the territory that is familiar to us. We know that
resistance doesn't serve us, yet it's difficult to let go of it, isn't it?
When there's anxiety involved, we tend to cling to our resistance:
"no, I don't want to go there!"

How do we work with resistance, then, when it arises? What if
we can't just relax or soften into it? First of all, let's return to the
message that may be trying to come through, using our skill of
listening to our anxiety...and to our resistance.

Embody the Resistance

Just as we listened to our anxiety, give your resistance an
opportunity to express itself. Resistance is simply another
layer of anxiety. If we don't acknowledge it, allow ourselves
to feel it, and listen to what it conveys, it's likely to stay
stubbornly in place.

Resistance isn't "bad," and not all resistance is problematic. It's important to discern whether this resistance is simply putting up needless roadblocks to your awakening or whether there's something significant going on here. So let's check it out.

Remember your skills of feeling your anxiety and listening to it. Apply this to whatever resistance arises in the process of transforming and releasing that anxiety. How do you feel the resistance in your body? Has it become tight and rigid? Or maybe you have become lethargic, heavy, or even immobile? Note whatever sensations are connected to it.

In fact, more than note the sensations—allow yourself to fully embody them. Does your body want to move or take a certain position? Maybe your arms want to push away at something, or your legs feel like running. Let yourself stand in place and run, or sit with your arms extended out in front of you, palms away. What actions, movements, or stances work for you to express that resistance?

The Message of the Resistance

Once you have allowed yourself to embody the movements and energy of the resistance, have a seat with a notebook and pen and invite your resistance to talk. You can even imagine that it is a character from a play or movie that you are meeting. Who or what does your resistance look like? How are they dressed, what are their expressions and mannerisms? Or maybe your resistance looks like an animal or an object. Is it a brick wall or a steel container? Let it be whatever it is, without judgment; just see what shows up in your mind's eye.

Give your resistance the floor. After all, it feels strongly about its objections, so you might as well hear them. Remember not to criticize or judge this resistance. Just jot down what it says or whatever it shows you. It may not convey its message in words, but in actions, images, sensations, symbols, sounds, or memories. Stay open; keep asking it how it feels and what it thinks, wants, and needs. Write it all down.

Your Protector

There may be good reason why resistance is arising. Anxiety arises because we don't feel safe. But it may also arise because we want to protect ourselves from dangerous situations, and stimulating the fear and worry will put us on guard. That's our protector within.

If resistance to releasing the anxiety shows up, it could be another layer of that inner protector. Remember how we explored in the "Empowering Action" chapter the way anxiety may be serving as a protector? Ask some similar questions of the resistance: "what are you trying to protect me from?" Ask it, or yourself, "What would be a more effective way of keeping yourself safe? What action would you like for me to take?" It's helpful to ask these questions again and again, digging a little deeper each time. The repetition allows you to peel away another layer of stress, worry, and that sense of being overwhelmed and find a bit more calm.

There's one more reason why resistance to releasing the anxiety may arise. As Leonard Jacobson, a well-known teacher of Presence, says in *Journey Into Now*, "If feelings like hurt, sadness, anger, and rage arise within you and you do not allow these feelings expression, then you might experience anxiety." By digging more deeply through feeling and listening to the resistance and asking these questions, those other emotions may

have permission and space to arise. Then, you can respond to
them compassionately and use the same keys to work through
those feelings as well.

Resilience Is the Opposite of Resistance

To let go of resistance, we move toward resilience. I like to
think of resilience as the opposite of resistance. In resistance,
we're fighting and pushing away the issue. We don't want to feel
anxiety. Make it go away! Resilience is the ability to hold our own
hand; to walk through the anxiety to the other side.

Resilience incorporates acceptance and surrender, but not
submission. We recognize the worries and fears that we're
feeling. We honor and acknowledge them—they came up for
a reason, and they are normal human emotions. Through the
practices and keys in this book, we have a process through which
we can work through the anxiety. We dive into and through
the wave. Then, we discover that we can deal with this. We're
capable, we're strong, we're empowered, and we can walk
through the stress and feelings of being overwhelmed. Resilience
means we don't need to avoid and run away; we have the
resources to walk through the territory. Usually we discover that
the experience of working through resistance leads us to far more
beautiful, lush, fertile land than we ever would have encountered
by taking the long path of avoidance around the anxiety.

Santosha—a Yogic Resilience Practice

Another gift from Yoga philosophy is helpful here—the practice (and state of mind) of *santosha* (pronounced sahn-TOE-shuh). Of all the elements of yoga philosophy, this one concept has probably had the biggest impact on my life (and it might for you, too, especially if you are a recovering perfectionist like me!).

Santosha translates as contentment. If you're the kind of person who loves excitement and adventure (I'm hearing the words of Yoda right now—"A Jedi craves not these things!"), contentment can sound pretty dull. I want to hold onto those highs, that drama, that ecstatic feeling of being in love, and even my artistic emotional angst.

First of all, not to worry. The surprising thing about *santosha* is that, in my experience, it is much more rewarding and joyful than the years when I rode the emotional roller coaster up and down in my life. Believe it or not, inner peace is deep, fulfilling, and immensely interesting.

But practicing contentment—which will increase emotional resilience significantly, thereby calming anxiety—does require us to loosen our grip on the two ends of the emotional spectrum.

What Is Contentment?

I think of *santosha*, the practice of contentment, as a foundation within us that's unshakable. It's that baseline of OK-ness, a deep inner knowing that whatever is happening, there's still a part of me that is all right. It is enough; it is sufficient to deal with whatever arises in every moment in life.

This taps directly back into the inner witness. Even in the midst of worry or upset, in the intensity of an emotional hurricane, we have the foundation laid that won't be blown over. I know that under that fear, some part of me is still OK. It may not feel like it's the majority of myself in the moment, but as I tap into the neutral, witnessing self, I feel an inkling of knowing the essence of who I am. That same, steady presence has always been within, and it is enough.

The Benefits of Contentment

Contentment has many benefits that return us to that state of calm, confidence, and courage.

1) It keeps us from swinging between highs and lows

Specifically in relation to anxiety, we may feel elated—but possibly deluded—when we believe we're safe. (There's that safety/danger polarity again!) We cling to the safety as well as the feeling of being on top of the world, thinking we have a handle on it all. But when something we perceive as "dangerous" shows up, we swing to the opposite experience of fear and despair. *Santosha* takes us to the fulcrum of the swinging pendulum and encourages a more calm, nonattached perspective.

2) It turns us inward to find our happiness, comfort, and ease

Swami Satchidananda says of contentment in his translation of *The Yoga Sutras of Patanjali*: "Contentment means just to be as we are without going to outside things for our happiness." When we let go of looking for conditions in our life to be completely safe, we find that our essence within provides us with the feeling of ease we're looking for. That feeling of ease

and comfort comes from doing the work of the seven keys
and developing the ability to be compassionately present with
ourselves through the anxiety.

3) It releases us from attachment (*raga*) and aversion (*dvesha*)

Remember when I first introduced attachment (*raga*) and
aversion (*dvesha*) in Chapter 4? Clinging to what we think
makes us feel safe and secure is attachment, and pushing our
anxiety away is aversion. The dynamic of conflict between
these opposing forces puts us in a perpetual spin of tension,
worry, and fear. We believe that we lack something that
will dispel our fears and that we have to get rid of whatever
disturbs us. As Baba Hari Dass states in his commentary on
the sutras, "Contentment means wanting nothing you don't
already have, and being satisfied with what you do have."
By cultivating contentment, we free ourselves from needing
anything other than what is here, right now, in this moment,
and discover that it is enough.

4) It changes our perspective

In *The Essence of Yoga*, Bernard Bouanchaud asserts:
"Contentment is a dynamic and constructive attitude that
brings us to look at things in a new way." We know that in
order to let go of anxiety and find our courage and confidence,
we have to learn to perceive situations, and even ourselves,
differently. From that foundation of contentment, we are able
to see that most of what scares us isn't real, that we're OK
somewhere inside ourselves, and that we're far more resilient
than we think we are.

The Strength in Vulnerability

One of the things that creates anxiety in us is the worry that we're too vulnerable. We believe that being vulnerable is weakness. This belief leads to the concern that if we're weak, we'll be unsafe; hence, the anxiety spikes.

But what is vulnerability, anyway? The concept of what it is to be vulnerable has gone through some transformation in the last decade or so. Those of us older than millennials associate the word with the traditional definition: capable of being physically or emotionally wounded, or open to being easily hurt or attacked. No one likes the idea of leaving themselves open for attack, and frankly, it's probably not wise.

That isn't the idea of vulnerability we're after. The traditional definition of vulnerability is more like foolishness. If we're constantly making ourselves open to attack, then we're probably not present and attentive. That kind of vulnerability is more likely to manifest when we are either out of our bodies or highly reactive.

However, when we're deeply grounded in our true Self, in our Divine presence within, very little is perceived as a threat. We know our source, we know that our thoughts aren't reality, and we have a deep connection with and trust in Spirit.

There's a new definition arising for what vulnerability means to us in this era—and it is especially relevant for overcoming anxiety. The Urban Dictionary reflects this shift in self-perception and consciousness. It defines vulnerable as: "Someone who is completely and rawly open, unguarded with their heart, mind, and soul. Being vulnerable happens when you trust completely."

Yes, vulnerability requires trust, as we explored in the "Surrender" chapter. And this is where we find the strength of being vulnerable. That unshakable trust is where we find our courage and calm. Remember *Ishvara Pranidhana*, the practice of deep trust and surrender to the Divine? Something greater than us causes the winds that fill our sails to blow. We can steer, but we rely on a greater force to carry us forward and to take us through the places that scare us.

Why Be Vulnerable?

I've made a case for how vulnerability has transformed in our modern culture, but you still may be wondering, "Why on earth would I want to be vulnerable? I don't want to be open and raw. How does it help me with my anxiety? Won't it just increase it?"

It could, if we used that vulnerability to reinforce the fearful thoughts that we could be harmed or attacked. But that's not how we're going to work with vulnerability in this case.

Vulnerability—the willingness to be that open and unguarded— allows us to be *real*. It is the gateway to the most authentic self within us. Brené Brown, professor at the University of Houston and lauded author of several bestselling books, including *The Gifts of Imperfection,* implores us all to embrace our most authentic selves. She defines authenticity as "the daily practice of letting go of who we think we're supposed to be and embracing who we are." A frequent trigger of anxiety is the belief that people will judge us or won't like us for who we are. So we hide behind a façade. We think it protects us, but it just reinforces our anxiety.

Being real and vulnerable gives others the opportunity to see and appreciate your true self. Building up the courage to be that authentic isn't easy. But remember that, the majority of the time, there isn't anyone out there judging us. *We* are judging us. *We* are making ourselves feel unsafe and open to attack by our beliefs and perceptions. And we have the power to change that. Through using the seven keys and beginning to perceive ourselves and the anxiety in a new way, we can take small steps toward sharing our feelings and our truth. When we do, we usually find out it's all right. We then build up the confidence to be more and more of who we truly are.

Fragility Is Precious

The truth is that there are fragile parts of ourselves. We can't deny that sometimes our feelings get hurt and our hearts get broken. It's part of being a human. But we can't go around defending ourselves to try to protect that fragile place inside. It merely perpetuates the anxiety.

Sometimes, we believe that we want to get rid of that fragility— make ourselves unbreakable, impenetrable. We don't like that fragility, and, like so many things that trigger our anxiety, we want to get rid of it.

But the fragile parts of ourselves are precious. Think about the beautiful things you use to decorate your home. Aren't some of the most beautiful art, flowers, crystals, and china fragile? Of course they are. Part of their beauty is how delicate they are. Do we just want to get rid of everything that is breakable, so we don't have to feel the disappointment and sadness if they crack or shatter? I know I don't. My daughter's pottery she made in fifth grade, my beautiful quartz crystal wand, a handblown glass dragonfly, the stained glass blue lotus hanging in my window: these things bring me inspiration and fill my heart.

Imagine what the world would be like without anything fragile or breakable. It would all be steel, concrete (arguably), or rubber. Nature wouldn't have flowers, delicate leaves, or mica. Not everything that appears fragile on the outside is weak, by the way. Think about a spider's web. To us, they're very delicate and fragile—we can easily run our hands through a spiderweb. But the spider's silk is five times as strong as the same weight of steel. There is beauty and hidden strength even in the most fragile, vulnerable parts of ourselves.

Wholeness Is Resilience

What I once again invite you to embrace is *wholeness*. You have incredibly powerful, strong, vibrant parts of yourself. You also have delicate, fragile, intricate, and serene aspects, and a myriad of other qualities and dimensions. Welcome it all in; give all parts of yourself safe space to be there, and as you do, you may begin to appreciate what you have judged or even feared.

The vulnerable, even fragile, parts within you contain your innocence, purity, joy, silliness, creativity, and playfulness. Within them reside the dancer or singer within you, as well as your tenderness and your willingness to speak up from your heart. Your vast, loving, compassionate, and passionate heart is held in your vulnerability. These places within you may feel fragile and get poked, or even shattered, sometimes.

But they are also the source of some of the most exquisite ways that you radiate and shine in the world. I wouldn't want you to lose your connection with those sacred and special places within you.

Remember That It's All Temporary

Even if a part of you feels like it is broken, it is temporary. You are not marred for life because of a past hurt or trauma. The only thing that is permanent is your Divine Self. You can heal and move past the anxiety and fear of being hurt again. You can integrate it into your wholeness as a small part of your story, one in which you have gained new understanding.

You don't have to be vulnerable all the time. Just because you have some fragility within you doesn't mean that is all you are. But by embracing those places inside rather than hiding or rejecting them, you become stronger. You develop resilience and recognize that you can take care of those sensitive aspects of yourself. You're so much more than any one quality or aspect.

Giving Birth to the New

By allowing this vulnerability to emerge from time to time, you become like a newborn again. Babies are definitely vulnerable. They are completely open and trusting, because they completely rely on their parents to care for them, unconsciously.

Human beings start this way; we are very vulnerable, and yet we are also tremendously resilient.

There is always something new wanting to be birthed within you, especially on this journey of transforming and releasing anxiety. You can't hold on to your old self if you want to step into being more calm, confident, and courageous. You'll need to let go, at least a little bit, and let the process birth you into who you are becoming. It's OK. Birth is a beautiful, powerful process. Allow yourself to see the new you emerging from this transformative experience.

Relax into the Process

Having given birth myself, I know that the most helpful practice during labor is to relax—which is a lot easier said than done! I clenched up in fear and became very tense in my body, which resulted in a longer labor. When I was able to relax more (yes, I did end up needing assistance for that!), my body opened up more and my daughter was able to emerge.

As the quote at the beginning of this chapter from one of my spiritual teachers, Amma (Mata Amritanandamayi), asserts, the more relaxed we can be in everything that we do, the better the results. We often think that the conditions need to be just so, and *then* we can relax. But that is an illusion. We can learn how to relax ourselves more and more by becoming present, developing embodiment, and surrendering into something that we trust. These practices not only help us calm down when our anxiety is triggered, but, done as part of our regular routine, they can help us cultivate a calm and ease that can accompany us into any situation.

Any time you can remember it, try to release your jaw and shoulders, soften your fists, and relax your belly. Touch your opposite hand or arm gently, with attention and compassion, and feel the soothing sense of the touch. Think of something that brings you peace, such as an alpine lake or a beautiful garden, and breathe slowly and deeply. Allow the thoughts to quiet like ripples on a pond slowly smoothing out into stillness. Give yourself many little breaks during the day to practice this

relaxation. From a more relaxed place, you'll find a reservoir
of resilience.

You can work through your resistance and find calm, confident
resilience. But if you find you're simply stuck in fear and don't
know what to do, read on. I've got your back.

Chapter 18

What to Do When You Feel Stuck

"Be patient with yourself. Self-growth is tender; it's holy ground. There is no greater investment."

—Stephen Covey

It's normal—anxiety will probably rear its head again. We are human beings, and we will still have our range of emotions. Hopefully by now, it won't have power over you like it did previously, and you can return to your inner calm and confident self. But what about when we feel stuck in that old fear, worry, and stress? What can we do if we don't feel like going through the steps in this book to find our way out of it?

As you journey forward on your path, have realistic expectations of yourself. You aren't going to be perfect. Remember that life, and spirituality, are messy. The first thing to remember is not to expect perfection of yourself. It is this very expectation—now, I should never feel anxiety again, and I shouldn't have to deal with this!—that *increases* the anxiety. Please, my friend, don't put that pressure on yourself. Instead, know that you have all the tools needed to release that anxiety and feel more relaxed. And if you're in a funk and can't seem to apply them, we have ways to get you back on track.

Here are my suggestions for what to do when you feel stuck in that anxiety again and you just can't seem to shake it off.

Remember that Self-Compassion Thingy?

Yeah, I know how it is—the anxiety comes up, and you think, arrrrgggggh! I have worked so hard on this and made such progress. I was peaceful and calm after meditating. My yoga practice was working, and I felt so relaxed. And now it's back!!!! I have failed!

I'm taking a deep breath for you—and please, join me and do the same. You haven't failed. You didn't do anything wrong. Please don't compare yourself to anyone else, or to how you were a week ago or even an hour ago. Just like the weather, emotions change and triggers can happen.

Let's remember the practice of self-compassion, the yogic practice of *karuna* turned toward yourself. I want that to be your go-to practice when you feel anxiety arise again. If you practice self-compassion, your inner self will then know you're safe. You see, if you attack yourself anytime you falter, the scared part of you is going to think you aren't a safe person. It's going to fear your judgment of that little girl or boy inside of you having a moment of fear. And as you can imagine, it's going to be tense, on edge, and more likely to feel anxious.

Embracing yourself with acceptance and self-compassion will go a long way towards softening the anxiety. OK, it's here again. I'm feeling nervous, I'm feeling scared. I'm going to stop for a moment and put my hands on my heart.

I want you to make yourself important enough to take the time to do that. You are worthy of that kindness and care. The time you take to be compassionate with yourself is most definitely worth it, because it will help you return to being your best self. Breathe as you touch your heart, and feel the anxiety. Tell yourself, "I can

see that you're suffering. You're feeling afraid. I understand, and
I'm right here for you."

Do your best, even if it isn't great—even if you struggle with
finding those self-compassionate words, and even if the kindest
thing you can think of to say is, "Well, whatever," or "I sure don't
like feeling this way." That's a start.

Imagine that you have the most compassionate, loving person
or deity ever in existence right next to you; it could be Jesus,
Mother Teresa, Quan Yin (the Asian goddess of compassion), or
your grandmother. When you think, "Now, that person is/was
really compassionate, kind, and caring," who comes to mind?
Notice who is in your thoughts when you muse, "They really
listened to me. They wouldn't judge me."

Bring them to mind, and then imagine what they would say to
you right now. Or, if you don't believe you deserve their time
and energy or kind words (we really can be hard on ourselves,
can't we?), what would they say to a crying baby, or a bystander
wounded in a war, or a victim of abuse?

Let those words be received by you. Write them down. Do not
compare your suffering to that of the victim of abuse—that's
not the point. Just use that scenario if you have a hard time
allowing yourself to receive the words directly. When you have
them written out, think about how you might change the wording
to fit your situation. You deserve to receive that compassion!
Remember that it is essential to be a good friend to yourself, to
practice *maitri*. Breathe it in, let it sink into every pore of your
body, feel it soaking into your heart and your soul. You are loved,
cared for, and understood.

The I Don't Wannas and the I Gotta Haves

Often, we just don't want something and we push it away—like our anxiety. Simultaneously, we also don't want to do anything about it; we avoid what we know will help. All that resistance is creating a pretty unpleasant environment in you, isn't it? In yogic philosophy, that resistance is called *dvesha*; dislike or aversion.

On the other end of the spectrum, we want something: "I've got to feel calm and relaxed! I need to feel more confident in this nerve-wracking situation." That is the force of attachment or desire, the counter-force to aversion. It's called *raga* in Sanskrit.

Raga and *dvesha* are two of the five causes of suffering in yoga philosophy. (You'll learn another one in the last chapter.) Here's one way to explain that suffering.

Have you ever been on a teacup ride at an amusement park? I grew up near Disneyland, and a few times a year I'd go there with my parents, or later as a teen with my friends. The teacup ride was especially fun for us as teens because we could make ourselves very dizzy, which made for a lot of laughter.

You sit inside the edges of the teacup, and in the center is a wheel. When the ride starts, you begin cranking the wheel around as fast as you can, which makes the teacup spin. How do you do that? Well, if you were just doing it for yourself, you'd pull on one side of the wheel with one hand and push away on the other side of the wheel with your other hand. You could also pull really hard toward you on one side, but the other side is always simultaneously moving away from you. That's what makes the wheel turn around—a combination of push and pull.

That's what you have going on with *raga* and *dvesha*. You are pushing something away with your thoughts: *I don't want that anxiety!* At the same time, you're trying to pull something toward you that you don't have: *I want calm!* What does that create? A spin! We run after one thing and run away from something else, around in a circle like a dog chasing its tail. This causes more anxiety for us (I want to feel safe *and* I don't want to be in danger) as well as perpetuates it.

By giving in to clinging to one thing, such as peace or confidence at the same time that we're pushing away our anxiety, we make ourselves spin out. It creates total agitation and restlessness, and the more we give in to *raga* and *dvesha*, the more these feelings are aggravated. This increases our suffering beyond the anxiety itself; we are trapped in wanting it to go away while wanting something else we don't have. I call it The I Don't Wannas and the I Gotta Haves.

How do we end the spin? Baba Hari Dass, yoga master and author of many books on yoga philosophy and practice, says, "In yoga, the mind is calmed by removing desires from the mind instead of fulfilling them. The anxiety of seeking is stopped, not because the object of desire is attained, but because the desire no longer exists." This is also affirmed by the Buddha in the second of his Four Noble Truths: "The root of suffering is *the attachment to the desire to have (craving, or raga) and the desire not to have (aversion, or dvesha).*"

To end the spin and release our anxiety, we have to stop investing in attachment to how we want things to be and aversion to what we don't like. We need to develop the neutral witness.

Step Back from Your Suffering—the Neutral Witness

It may be hard to believe, but the fact that you're noticing your anxiety is a step in the right direction. It's no longer unconscious. You're aware and awake now. I'm sure you noticed the fears before, but now you're probably very attuned to when they arise. That is helpful, because the sooner you notice what is going on, the sooner you can implement these tools and skills to shift that energy for the better.

Remember the inner witness from Chapter 8, where we practiced looking at ourselves from a little distance with a neutral attitude? The inner witness simply sees what is, without judgment. It is a *neutral* witness. When you have some part of you that can step into neutrality for a bit, you give yourself some space to choose. Simply watch the play of *raga* and *dvesha*, or the anxious thoughts themselves. You can choose to keep thinking those thoughts and investing in attachment and aversion, or you can think of something else to focus on.

When you step back from the anxiety through neutral witnessing, something else may start to feel more possible. This is the time to pull out the different tools we have developed through this book and select one to work with. What feels doable? Could you take some time to get centered and grounded, maybe even step outside and put your feet on the earth? Are you present in this moment? You could focus on your breath or a picture hanging on the wall, slowly and mindfully eat a handful of raisins, or put some music on and listen to the soothing sound. The more you can focus on something else—especially through your senses, in the present moment—the more you will weaken the feeling of anxiety.

Acknowledge What You *Are* Doing

Taking the role of the neutral witness of your experience also allows you to recognize what you *are* doing to alleviate your anxiety. When we receive acknowledgment, it feels pretty good, doesn't it? But when you feel anxiety and don't feel like dealing with it, you're probably berating yourself rather than acknowledging yourself.

What have you been applying from what you know? You're reading this book, that's a good start. You've been willing to work on your worries and fears. Have you taken a few deep breaths? Good. Given yourself a few kind and compassionate thoughts? Great, that's progress. Did you have some times when you weren't feeling anxious, or when you were able to shift yourself out of it? I'd say you're doing quite well. This is just a temporary setback.

Acknowledging yourself is affirming that you are already enough, even if the anxiety arises. You have enough information and tools. You're capable, and you can do this. Your Divine self is full and complete within you, always, and you have what you need. It's just a matter of making the connections, practicing, and learning to access the inner calm, steadiness, and stability that are already deep within you.

Remember Your Boundaries

It is entirely possible that the anxiety has surfaced again because you took on someone else's stuff. If it isn't your own emotions, energies, or issues and you clearly recognize that, it will be easier to let go of the anxiety.

Review the practices on energetic boundaries in the "Embodiment" chapter. What is *you*, and what is *not you*? If something you saw on the news or YouTube disturbed you, acknowledge that it's out there, but it's not in your personal environment at this moment. If a friend just dumped all their worries on you, you can be compassionate, but don't be a sponge for their miseries. It's not necessary for you to absorb their feelings and process them through your whole body, thereby disturbing your feeling of calm and well-being. If it's something that you care dearly about and want to initiate change, you'll be far more effective if you don't recreate all the suffering you see or hear about in your own body.

Think about an emergency response worker. How do you think they are trained? Imagine what it would be like if they arrived on the scene, took in all the pain and fear they're seeing, and had a freak-out? Not very effective, eh? They have to have very clear energetic boundaries around themselves and be determined not to take in everyone's pain, or they won't be able to help a soul. It is essential that they stay centered, grounded, and clear about who they are and what they're there to do so they can move people to safety, treat wounds, put out fires, and care for those in grief.

So keep other people's stuff out on the outer edge of your energetic boundary. When you stay clear in your own energetic field, you'll be able to respond from your center rather than reacting from your anxiety. You'll still register that it's there, but honestly, don't pile more on top of your own worries!

Want a couple secret weapons to employ when you just don't know what to do to get your anxiety under control? Read on!

Secret Weapon Number 1— Play!

It may be the last thing you think of when you're feeling anxiety, but one very effective tool—if you're willing to use it—is to have fun. Playfulness is an excellent antidote to both resistance and fear. Can you picture yourself being silly, laughing, having fun, *and* being fearful and worried at the same time? Pretty hard to do, isn't it? OK, maybe you're one of those talented folks who can do both. But if you were fully invested in enjoying yourself, don't you think it would be tough to hold on to the fear?

It doesn't work in all situations, but sometimes you can shift the energy and take yourself at least partially out of the fears with playfulness. It helps you move through resistance, too. Put on some of your favorite tunes and dance around the room (don't worry, I'm not looking). Go in the bathroom and make the silliest faces you can in the mirror. Shake your booty! Scream, shout, bark like a dog, I don't care—anything that moves your energy. Scribble all over a piece of paper with lots of colors. Find something engaging, let loose, and have fun!

Take your lesson from young children. This is what they do to get their energy out and how they shift themselves out of being upset. They might cry for a couple minutes, reach for their mother, and seek some comfort after they have fallen and skinned a knee. Then, they get up and go back to playing, and, in short order, they're done with it. We adults like to sit around, obsess, mope, and review the whole concern over and over—no wonder we have anxiety issues! In fact, if you have a child, take some time out to play with them, preferably outside. See what happens with your anxiety.

You know what almost always shifted my daughter and I out of agitation or a bad mood? Taking a running leap and jumping onto the bed in our master bedroom. We'd alternate flying through the air and landing with our faces smashed into the pillows. We'd see how far each of us could leap across the bed, and sometimes we held hands and did it together. After a few minutes, we were breathless and giggly.

One thing I have found is that when my anxiety is running high, I'm forgetting to have fun in my life. I become too serious and allow the things that bring me joy and laughter to fall off my list. Have you become too serious or forgotten how to play? Make sure that having fun has a space in your life. It helps to balance out our fears and worries.

What are some pastimes that are fun for you? Make a list of them. Include activities that you can do on the spot, like jump rope or doodling, as well as other interests that might involve a field trip, like playing tennis with a friend, going for a swim, or watching a comedy. Playfulness and having fun are powerful secret weapons to overcome your anxiety.

Secret Weapon Number 2— The Patronus Exercise

Let's say that you're having a hard time getting some distance— moving into the space of that neutral witness—from your fearful thoughts. It's difficult to set your boundaries, and you just can't seem to enjoy yourself. At this point, it's time to use some magic. Using this powerful visualization may be enough to give you a leg up on that anxiety.

This takes its inspiration from the Harry Potter series—have you read it or seen the movies? One of its most potent magical spells calls forth your *Patronus*. As author J.K. Rowling describes it, the Patronus is "a kind of positive force, a projection of hope, happiness, [and] the desire to survive." The Patronus doesn't feel fear and despair the way humans do.

Its function is to protect you from the Dementors. In the Harry Potter books, the Dementors are dark ghoul-like beings that suck all the positive, happy memories and energy out of you. Yikes, right? That's what your anxiety is like! It drains your positive energy and makes you forget about your courage, strength, capability, and the times when you've felt calm and confident.

Well, wizards and witches aren't the only ones who have a Patronus—you do, too! It's the aspect of your inner self that believes in you, that holds your memories of happiness and ease, and that sees the magical possibilities of life. You can ward off fears and negativity when you're tuned into your Patronus. And it can even repel your very own frightening, disturbing thoughts.

The essential practice when you feel your own Dementors of anxiety raising their terrifying heads is to recognize that they are *thoughts* and don't really have power over you unless you *give* it to them. The magical force of the Patronus acts as a shield, helping you to refocus on what is positive in your life rather than allowing the anxiety to drag you down. It creates a force field around you that literally repels and tosses those Dementors away!

I think the Patronus exercise is fun and beautiful. If you're a visual person and enjoy using imagery, it may be just the secret weapon you've been looking for.

The Patronus is a luminescent, glowing white light in the form of an animal—your own personal power animal to repel that anxiety. Choose an animal that speaks to your heart and soul. Is it a stag, like Harry Potter's? How about a dolphin, or your beloved cat or dog? What about an eagle? Select a creature that resonates for you to represent your Patronus, or let one spontaneously come to you!

When those negative thoughts arise, cast your spell. You can use the Latin words for the spell: *Expecto Patronum!* Imagine your Patronus, glowingly radiant and mighty, making a stand between you and the illusory fears. And just like the Dementors, see those thoughts and fears repelled away.

OK, I know it's not always that easy to dissipate anxiety. But with this fun exercise, you'll be less intimidated by your fears and worries. It is one more tool to have in your pocket (along with your wand, of course) that will help you transform anxiety into something more helpful and uplifting.

With the aid of your Patronus, you can gain some distance from your anxious thoughts, utilize the other tools we've explored to dismantle them, and find empowerment over them. Imagining your Patronus and the shield it puts between you and your worries gives you a little space to examine the anxiety. Do a reality check: are the fearful thoughts true? Are they necessary? Do I really need to let them have power over me? No, you don't.

Expecto Patronum! You've got this!

Patience—Everything Changes

When you feel anxiety coming on and getting you into a stuck place, remember that everything changes. It is essential to have patience with this process. Part of what creates anxiety is expecting things to change immediately. Impatience is another hallmark of a high-anxiety person. We can't tolerate it, it's too scary, it must stop now! When you recognize that this won't last forever and that it will eventually improve if you're patient, your nervous system can relax a bit.

I'll say it again: *everything in the universe changes.* Nothing stays the same forever. This fact is where the old adage, "This too shall pass," originates. If you stay with the feelings mindfully, being open, present, and compassionate, they will shift.

Recall the exercises from the "Feeling Your Anxiety" chapter. Chances are very good that if you stay with it, breathe into it, and allow yourself to feel the stress (rather than *think* about it), it's going to change. It might get worse for a little bit. But I guarantee you that it won't stay there forever.

Remember, though, that trying to resist it (there's *dvesha* again!) keeps refueling the very thing you don't want. So if you sit with the anxiety with the expectation, "I'm going to make this go away by feeling it," it won't be very effective. We need to be willing, interested, and caring about the part of ourselves that feels anxious, and we need to trust the process. *Listen* to the anxiety. Wait for the message or the shift. Be patient.

I'll say it again—trust the process! The anxiety can lead you to more resilience and courage in facing whatever arises in life. It can initiate your greater spiritual awakening. Continue to walk steadily on the path to more ease, inner peace, and confidence.

Chapter 19

Seeing through the Anxiety to Your Self

"Who sees all beings in his own self, and his own self in all beings, loses all fear."

—Isa Upanishad

I'm delighted to see you've arrived at the last chapter—and I'll bet you are, too. You've come a long way through this exploration and gained many tools and skills to transform your anxiety into a more easeful, confident way of living. By now, you should have a clear idea of what you might be doing to exacerbate your anxiety, how to change that, and how to feel more calm and confident in your life.

I want to remind you of some important concepts to make your practice more gentle, more fun, and easier as you work with the steps of practice and nonattachment, presence, embodiment, self-compassion, feeling your anxiety, listening to your anxiety, empowering actions, and surrender. Let's reflect back on those mis-takes that people on the spiritual path tend to encounter and remember how to respond in a way that will transform your anxiety rather than perpetuate it.

Practice Imperfectly

Yes, I know that you might want to fall back into old habits and try to do all of these steps perfectly. I find myself still wanting to do this, too. We figure that if we can do everything just right, then we can *abolish* that anxiety!

But by now, you understand that any approach that tries to make anxiety go away—especially if it tries to get rid of it fast—will likely backfire on you. Remember, that is a sneaky way of doing violence to yourself. You don't want to reject any part of you that feels fear. You want to love, hold, and listen to it until it releases of its own will. Then, the anxiety won't hold power over you. You'll know you can deal with it. That's resilience.

So let yourself try out these concepts, and, yes, make mis-takes ! Guess what? When you give yourself permission to make mis-takes , your anxiety automatically decreases. Another counterintuitive strategy that works!

Your Anxiety Isn't "Bad"

Remember that the fears aren't bad, awful emotions—they actually have a message. By feeling and listening to your anxiety rather than judging it, you'll be able to use anxiety to inform your responses to the world. You'll no longer need to run from life.

Instead of "flight to the light" and avoiding the "dark" places in you that scare you, get to know them. Do some inner scuba diving, and seek to understand your shadow self. True safety isn't fleeing into the light; it's knowing that you can handle whatever might be there in the darkness. Rather than flight to the light, think of it as bringing the light of wisdom and understanding into the dark, "scary" places.

Get to Know Your Body—and Live in It!

Now you know that you don't need to leave your body to feel safe. In fact, you know that by developing more presence and embodiment, you'll feel more at home in the world and more capable of responding to the challenges that bring up fear and feelings of being overwhelmed.

Feeling at home in your body is exquisite. There's so much joy and aliveness to be found in each moment. You'll delight in your yoga practice, walking, hiking, feeling your breath, and attuning to the sensations of gliding through water as you swim. You can relish your senses when you feel at home in your body and have more enjoyment from a sweet and tart strawberry and a piece of chocolate melting on your tongue (I just had to throw some chocolate in there!).

When your body knows you appreciate it and are fully present, it relaxes. It's so good to know that someone is home, isn't it?

Maintain Healthy Energetic Boundaries

I know you care about the state of the world, the animals at the shelter, and your family and friends. But you don't need to feel and absorb all their suffering just to show that you care. And it's not more spiritual to take on their pain, either. It disturbs your health, your heart, your energy, and your peace of mind.

Remember to meet the suffering that you see with your compassionate attention. But keep it outside of your energy field, where you can sense and feel it but not run it through your nervous system. Trust in the process, offer your prayers or your helpful actions, do your "Me/Not Me" practice, and let it go. Your body and your psyche will thank you for this.

Be Compassionate to Yourself and Let Go

You can enjoy creating your life and manifesting more calm, peace, and ease—just as long as you surrender attachment to the results and forgive yourself when things don't go as planned. Let go of the pride/shame polarity; don't get cocky and think that now you've got this totally handled. Don't freak out when things fall apart. Find the middle way, or transcend both ends by surrendering your expectations.

You know that life isn't "perfect" even for those who have supposedly mastered the Law of Attraction. At times, the Divine may have something else in mind for you. It may not appear on the surface to be the desired outcome, but it might have hidden gifts.

Often, when we gain competency in a skill, the Universe responds by upping the ante. We are met with a situation that is more challenging, that might bring up anxiety again. You didn't do anything wrong—in fact, it's a sign that *you're getting the hang of this*. Spirit thinks you can handle more.

There is no need to feel like a failure or ashamed for "creating" this. You have a new opportunity to expand your skills, have more compassion for yourself, and surrender everything you can to something greater. Open to your guidance and empowering actions; you can trust in Spirit to show you the way through the anxiety back to the quiet, serene place inside you—again and again.

Embrace How It Is

As you develop your neutral witness and nonattachment to the outcome of situations and your efforts, you'll naturally feel less anxious. You can begin to see that life flows and has ups and downs. It is neither safe nor dangerous, although it can appear to be either at any given moment, depending on your point of view. What point of view will you choose?

When you feel the polarity of dangerous vs. safe showing up, consider your empowering action. What response will take you out of the polarity and into flowing with the present moment? What action or new perspective will support you better in managing the challenges of the moment? How can you care for yourself through the situation without deciding that it's too scary?

If it's a *known* fear, take action to get to safety. But if it's an *unknown* fear, and you recognize that you're *imagining* the worst, in that moment, you can choose to step out of that train of thought. A higher order is at hand here. Surrender to your higher power. You can allow that to carry you through, rather than putting all your energy into how dangerous it might be and what will make you feel safer.

Truth vs. truth

The final step on this journey out of living in anxiety and into living in freedom is distinguishing truth from untruth. The anxiety is, as many of our perceptions are, an illusion. It is a distorted way of viewing the world and is not based on reality. Anxiety is based on our beliefs *about* reality.

In order to talk about reality, we need to distinguish between what I call "truth" with a lower case "t" and Truth with a capital "T." Both are important on the journey from anxiety to ease and inner peace.

The small "t" truth refers to *changing truth*. These are the various conditions and experiences we have from day to day. In this moment, it may be 50 degrees outside as you read this. That is true—the temperature is what it is in that given moment. But of course, one hour or several hours later, that temperature can go up or down. This is the changing truth.

You may feel anxiety in this moment. That experience is true. But it doesn't stay the same, does it? It might intensify, or it might disappear altogether. Your emotions, sensations, thoughts, and experiences all fall into the category of small "t," ever-changing truth.

When we're looking at truth that changes, we also learn to use our wisdom to distinguish what is truth and what is interpretation. 50 degrees is 50 degrees: to someone from Alaska, that may be T-shirt weather. But someone from Brazil may be bundled up in a sweater and a jacket. One feels warm, the other cold. *Our interpretation or perception of the changing truth is not the same as something actually being true.*

This is essential with transforming our anxiety. When we see a snake, we may feel fear. But first of all, is it really a snake, or is it just a rope on the ground? I'm sure you've heard that metaphor before. But let's say that it really is a snake—that is true. Does that mean we are in danger, that there is something to fear? In reality, it doesn't. It could be a garter snake, which is essentially harmless. It could be a rattlesnake, but it may have no interest in hurting you. It could be at a distance from you, say on the other side of a road, well out of your reach. But our anxiety believes that it is a dangerous situation, and so we believe that is true.

What is true is that we are feeling anxiety; what is not true is the perception that the situation is dangerous. When we can reality check ourselves like this and distinguish small "t" truth from perception and interpretation, we can downshift our anxiety to a less tense response.

Large "T" Truth

Truth with a capital T is the *unchanging truth*. It is the spiritual reality that underlies everything in existence. According to the ancient sages, especially from Hindu tradition and yoga philosophy, that unchanging truth is Consciousness. It is our essence, our true nature. This Truth does not change but is the eternal witness that observes everything in the universe birthing, coming into form, and dissolving back into Spirit again.

Understanding this principle—and beginning to live it—will dramatically change how you work with your anxiety and may be the ultimate key to releasing it.

You are not your thoughts, emotions, or sensations. You have a body, but you are not the body. The ultimate spiritual truth is that we are pure awareness; part of the one Consciousness that gives rise to and is in everything. This is the Truth that the ancient sages have always known and endeavored to awaken us to.

When we know that we are this infinite Consciousness, the anxiety can only have power over us if we choose to give it that power. We may still experience the anxiety, but knowing this Truth strips it of the ability to consume us. We can witness it as another emotion or thought rising and falling, but our witness self is the Truth of our being.

Anxiety as Your Messenger

When anxiety arises, we can look at it as our messenger. It is asking us to do a reality check: is this fear about something real (known fear) or illusory (unknown fear)? If we look at our fears from the perspective of capital "T" Truth, we see that most of them are not real. The only thing that is ultimately real—unchanging Truth—is Consciousness.

The anxiety shows up to reveal what is false. Your spiritual opportunity is to call it like it is—to call out your illusory fears, knowing that they can't stand up to the litmus test. You can look at the anxiety as a friendly adversary that is going to test you and keep you on your path of Truth, if you allow it to.

So when the worries arise, put *them* to the test: question their truth, and continually realign yourself with the Truth that you are one with the infinite presence, which isn't subject to fear (especially about what isn't actually happening *now*).

Shrinking Your Fear Back Down to Size

When we whittle our fears and worries down to the most basic fear, it's usually the fear of death. This is known in yogic philosophy as *abhinivesha* (another one of the five causes of suffering). Anxiety becomes so big because, unconsciously, we're taking it to the extreme—we fear obliteration and devastation.

Why are we afraid to speak in public? Underneath the worry that people will laugh, judge us, and throw tomatoes, or that we'll become embarrassed, it is a fear of death—that our sense of self will be devastated—that drives the intensity of this anxiety. You can take almost any anxiety issue and trace it back to some variation of *losing ourselves*.

The fear that we will cease to exist when the physical body dies is universal. But it's misleading, if we're spiritually aware. On the spiritual path, we know that who we truly are—Truth—is Divine, unchanging, eternal. But we still constantly operate as if we don't know that, because we haven't realized it: we haven't made it *real* to ourselves.

It's probably too big of a stretch for most of us to simply recognize that, hey, we don't really die, so why be afraid? But what we *can* do is recognize that most anxiety-provoking situations aren't going to result in obliteration. Even if you're not fearing death per se, but rather a devastation of your sense of self or how people perceive you, you might be blowing the situation up to be a lot bigger than it actually is. And hence, your anxiety becomes a lot bigger than it needs to be.

Acknowledge when you're making your fears much bigger than is called for by the actual circumstances. When we stress out about meeting a deadline or others' expectations and the anxiety

goes through the roof, we can remember *this isn't life or death.*
I'm not going to die from finishing the project a day late, hurting
someone else's feelings, or disappointing my boss. It might be
uncomfortable and upsetting, but it isn't life or death. We can
recognize when we're invoking *abhinivesha* (pronounced like
uh-bee-nee-VAY-shuh), the fear of death, and making life a lot
scarier than it needs to be.

You're Bigger Than the Anxiety

Just as there is a greater Truth than the temporary fluctuation
of events and experiences, there is a greater *you* beyond your
sense of self. Small "s" self is your personality or ego, which we've
explored. Your capital "S" Self is your transcendent self and is
one with the Universe.

We all know we have the small "s" self, even if we don't think
about it. That's who you refer to as yourself. We identify
ourselves, for example, as female, male, tall or short, quirky,
enthusiastic, quiet, hardworking, a business owner, a nurse, a
particular cultural background, age, and so on.

As a spiritual person, you also know that your soul or spirit is
beyond all that—it is the capital "S" self that is transcendent,
unlimited, and one with the Divine. If you didn't already know
that, I'm here to tell you: that is your true nature!

What's really powerful about recognizing both our smaller self
and our larger Self is that it can shift you out of anxiety. Our
small self is the one that becomes afraid. But in our large Self, we
are much bigger than our fears. Our Self can hold all the worries,
stress, and sense of being overwhelmed and not only know that it
is temporary but remain aware that we are completely capable of

walking through it all. By being in our Self, we shrink the anxiety down to its proper small size, and we know the greatness of who we truly are.

Dodging Bullets?

Shrinking your anxiety down to a realistic size—maybe I'm nervous about a presentation, but I'll be OK—is a superpower you can have with the knowledge of Truth and the application of the skills in this book. But it isn't about dodging bullets. It doesn't mean that when anxiety comes up, you will be able to escape it at lightning speed.

Did you ever see the movie, *The Matrix*? In it, Morpheus, the wise mentor, advises Neo, the hero-in-the-making, about his latent gifts that he hasn't yet discovered. Neo has the ability to see through all the illusion in the world and transcend it. But he hasn't realized it yet. Morpheus is there to convince him that he will.

Neo says, "What are you trying to tell me? That I can dodge bullets?" And Morpheus responds: "No, Neo. I'm trying to tell you that when you're ready, *you won't have to*."

We spend all of our lives trying to dodge these bullets of our fears and worries. We think that by avoiding them, we'll get over them. But the problem with that is that we still buy into the bullets. We still believe that the fears are being shot at us, they're dangerous, they can kill us, and we've got to get away from them. Is that really freedom?

No, it's not. It's just a more attractive way to wrap up the package of our fear, the idea that we can skirt around it so it won't kill us. We still believe it *could* kill us, which is not a great way to live.

Trying to make the anxiety go away or dodge it perpetuates the very thing that amps it up: the belief that you can't deal with it or that there's something wrong with you that you have it.

When we hold fast to the deeper Truth—that the fears are, for the most part, illusory, and there is something much greater within us that transcends them—we don't have to dodge bullets. Just like in the movie, we'll see through the illusion of the bullets and perceive that the anxiety is thought, not reality. The bullets dissolve, and all that remains is the awareness of the thoughts.

It's another perspective that comes from the *neutral witness* practice: seeing things as they are gives you some distance from them and a new perspective, and it disarms the fear. The bullets no longer have power over you.

You are a Divine being. As you realize that more and more, you have access to whatever you need from the Universe. You can open yourself to unlimited strength, courage, inspiration, and resilience. Just as there is access to light, love, and peace from the Divine, you can call forth whatever you need to support you through the fear and release it from you. After you've done all the work in this book, this will be your final and biggest step to live a life of more calm, confidence, and courage.

You are ready, and you can do it! You're much bigger than this fear. Everything is available to you if you're open, willing, and receptive. As you open more to being your Divine self, you'll see through the illusion of your fears more clearly and more often. And you'll know inside that you already have what you need and already are what you long to be. It's here, right now, in this present moment.

I wrote this book for you, and I see it in you, as I see it in the eyes of every being I have encountered. I will continue to hold for you this true vision of yourself. Step by step, I know that you are getting closer to knowing that truth for yourself and knowing that anxiety no longer defines who you are. See your *Self*, know your *Self*, and be your *Self*, and then your *Self* will be in charge, not your anxiety.

Recommended Reading

The Highly Sensitive Person by Elaine N. Aron

The Life Visioning Process by Michael Bernard Beckwith

Spiritual Liberation by Michael Bernard Beckwith

When Things Fall Apart by Pema Chodron

The Yoga Sutras of Patanjali by Baba Hari Dass

Infinite Possibilities by Mike Dooley

The Big Leap by Gay Hendricks

Journey Into Now by Leonard Jacobson

The 5 Personality Patterns by Steven Kessler

Self-Compassion: The Proven Power of Being Kind to Yourself by Kristin Neff

The Four Agreements by Don Miguel Ruiz

The Voice of Knowledge by Don Miguel Ruiz

The Marriage of Spirit by Leslie Temple-Thurston

Patanjali's Yoga Sutras: Gateway to Enlightenment by Rama Jyoti Vernon

Acknowledgments

Without my husband's encouragement to take a powerful course in writing a book in just three months, this book probably would never have existed. Thank you, Michael, for always believing in me. And thank you, Meera, my dear daughter, for your understanding and putting up with my many days and nights of click-click-clicking on the keyboard.

And thank you to Angela Lauria, who pushed, prodded, kept me on track, and created a method of writing that allowed the words to flow like a river.

My deepest gratitude to all the students, clients, and colleagues whose experiences of growth contributed to this book. It has been an honor to accompany you. Thank you for sharing and being willing to dive deep into yourself.

There are many others who have helped bring this book into the world. Thank you to Lynda Caesara and Steven Kessler, whose feedback and suggestions were immensely helpful. To Syl Sabastian for your immense support throughout. And big hugs and thank you to my amazing book launch team! In alphabetical order: Tim Custis, Darlene Frank, Melissa Harrison, Sonya Kelly, Jeanie Lerner, Sylvia Mitulescu, Holly Devi Moore, Deborah Raphael, Syl Sabastian, Kai Seidenburg, Annie Talbot, Chitra Vivek, Janne Wallace, Jeff Wegner, and Jessica Zerr. Your support has contributed greatly to the success of this endeavor. I deeply appreciate your feedback and encouragement along this path.

Finally, I wish to honor some of my many teachers along the way: Leslie Temple-Thurston and Brad Laughlin, from whom I continue to learn the neutral witness and the most powerful synthesis of yoga philosophy and psychology I have found; Lynda Caesara, my energy work teacher, who truly taught me embodiment; Leonard Jacobson, my Presence teacher, who opens my heart and quiets my mind without a word; and to my longtime teacher, Amma, the embodiment of love, service, and compassion—words cannot express my gratitude. Thank you for showing me what is possible, holding my hand, and reminding me every day that nothing matters more than love.

Thank You

It brings me great joy to share this book with you, and I hope you've found it helpful in transforming anxiety into a life of more happiness, calm, and ease. I'd love to hear from you! Please send me your feedback, questions, insights, and challenges, and I'll write you back: Connie@AwakeningSelf.com.

Do you wonder if you really have anxiety? Could the very things you're doing to calm your stress and anxiety—like yoga, affirmations, or meditation—actually be *making it worse*? I've created a free assessment to find out. You'll also receive a free Q & A class, too! Take your assessment at my website:

www.AwakeningSelf.com/awakening-from-anxiety/anxiety-assessment

About the Author

Rev. Connie L. Habash

Rev. Connie L. Habash, MA, LMFT, has been passionate about personal and spiritual growth since the age of eleven, when she just *knew* that The Force really existed. Since then, her journey has not only taken her deeply into her spirituality, but also through her own personal healing of anxiety and depression, as well as supporting hundreds of others in transformation and awakening.

Many fields interested her in college, including the humanities, drama, languages, and social studies. But an epiphany revealed that psychology brought them all together. In 1987, she received her BA in Psychology from UC Irvine, followed by a Master's in Counseling Psychology from JFK University in 1994, and became licensed as a Marriage and Family Therapist in 1999.

Her personal path has taken her through many spiritual traditions, including earth-based spirituality, Taoism, African traditions, mystical Christianity, Buddhism, and her greatest love, Hinduism and yoga philosophy. Connie discovered yoga in 1991, and she immediately knew she wanted to teach; two years later, that dream was realized. Her love of universal spiritual principles led her to seek ordination as an Interfaith minister in 2012.

Rev. Connie regularly facilitates classes, spiritual community gatherings, women's groups, yoga teacher trainings, and retreats, and has a counseling practice in Menlo Park, CA. She "blogs on Psych Central," has been quoted in the *Huffington Post*, *Reader's Digest*, NBCNews.com, and Thriveworks, and has articles in Elephant Journal and on *New York Times* bestselling author Mike Dooley's TUT website. Her orientation toward personal and spiritual growth integrates body, mind, heart, and spirit with her years of experience on the yoga mat and in the therapist chair.

When Connie isn't seeing clients or teaching, she can be found spending time with her family, sitting (or weeding!) in her garden, hiking in the redwoods, or cuddling with her cat, Milo.

Rev. Connie offers a powerful online program based on this book; if you'd like to have her personal guidance through the keys explained here and make a shift out of anxiety into more calm and confidence, contact her at Connie@AwakeningSelf.com.

Website: www.AwakeningSelf.com
Facebook: www.facebook.com/AwakeningSelf